$\mathfrak{A}$
DISPENSATIONAL
TRUTH

REFUTING THE MYTH THAT
DISPENSATIONALISM IS NEW

JAMES C. MORRIS

DISPENSATIONAL
PUBLISHING HOUSE, INC.

Printed in the United States of America

First Edition, First Printing, 2018

ISBN: 978-1-945774-29-4

Dispensational Publishing House, Inc.
PO Box 3181
Taos, NM 87571

www.dispensationalpublishing.com

This is a DPH Quick Print book. Our QuickPrint process allows us to get books to the market at a much quicker pace and lower cost than the full book publishing process. If you discover errors in this book, please contact the publisher so that these errors may be fully removed in future editions.

Ordering Information:
Quantity sales. Special discounts are available on quantity purchases by churches, associations, and others. For details, contact the publisher at the address above.

Orders by U.S. trade bookstores and wholesalers. Please contact the publisher:
Tel: (844) 321-4202

1 2 3 4 5 6 7 8 9 10

This book is dedicated to the Lord Jesus Christ, the only Son of the only God, without whose sacrifice at Calvary this book would be both pointless and impossible. It is also dedicated, in a lessor sense, to those that backed the writer with prayer during the years of research and writing that went into it, and to his beloved wife Fina, who lovingly cared for him throughout this time.

Table of Contents

PREFACE

Many attempt to discredit dispensationalism by claiming that the church never taught it before around 1830. Such a claim is ridiculous, for proof that any particular idea was never taught in any particular time period would require an exhaustive examination of every teaching that took place during that period. Even for a relatively short period of time, such an exhaustive search is manifestly impossible, much less for nearly eighteen centuries.

But this claim involves a serious falsehood. This is that the accuracy or error of a doctrine can be determined on the basis of how long men have taught it. On the surface, this notion seems obvious, because surely the godly men of ages past must have studied the scriptures extensively, and had to have been well acquainted with what they say. But when people think like this, they forget that almost all of the great scholars of the scriptures who lived in the time of Jesus were ignorant of much of what their own scriptures said about the coming of their great Messiah. These scriptures presented two apparently contradictory pictures of this promised Messiah. Some of them portrayed Him as a great conquering hero who would live forever. And others portrayed Him as a meek, suffering servant, who would die for his people. Since they liked the great conquering hero parts, they studied them at length, and almost totally ignored the meek suffering servant parts. So when their Messiah came as a meek, suffering servant, they did not recognize Him, and fulfilled the parts about his death, down to the tiniest detail.

Even so, men of all ages have had similar prejudices, which have blinded them to significant portions of God's Holy Word, the Bible. We have no right to base our ideas on anything other than the word of God itself. Anything less that this is a false foundation.

But this claim, as well as being both ridiculous and based on a false concept, is simply not correct. In 2015 a study[1] was published by William C. Watson, in which he traced a very large number of dispensational concepts, including a few cases of full dispensationalism, that were published in the English language long before the 1800s.

Watson's study covered mainly a period of about a hundred and fifty years shortly following the publication of the King James Translation of the Bible. This had, for the first time in history, made complete Bibles readily available in the common language at a price ordinary people could afford. The result was a veritable explosion of Bible study and commentary throughout the English speaking world. So, about 30 years later, in the 1640s, many commentaries began to appear in the English language. These, based on scripture, rather than on what "scholars" had taught, contained a huge amount of truth that had long been forgotten.

Of course, those who disparage dispensationalism with the claim that it is a relatively modern "invention," will simply argue that, although Watson has moved the marker back a few hundred years, dispensationalism still could not even possibly be true because it was never taught before the date of Watson's earliest example. But that would also be incorrect.

Contrary to the claims of the detractors of these truths, dispensationalism was not even new at that time. It was only restored at that time. Both

---

1 Dispensationalism Before Darby: Seventeenth-Century and Eighteenth-Century English Apocalypticism," By William C. Watson, Silverton, OR 97381, ISBN 978-1-942614-03-6.

the general idea of dispensationalism itself, and most of its important details, were clearly taught in truly ancient Christian writings.

The purpose of the present study is to examine numerous instances of dispensational doctrine that were clearly taught in some of the very oldest Christian writings on Bible prophecy that have survived to the present day, as well as in numerous other truly ancient Christian writings.

While there were indeed a few earlier Christian writers that had made a few comments relative to Bible prophecy, the earliest Christian known to modern scholars who wrote at length about Bible prophecy was Papias.[2] The famous church historian Eusebius, who wrote in the mid fourth century, complained about how "many of the Christian writers after him adopted a like opinion"[3] to that of Papias, and gave Irenaeus as an example of these "many" writers. So we know that this writer, whose work has been lost, taught ideas at least somewhat similar to those we will soon examine.

The very oldest Christian commentary on Bible prophecy that has survived to the present day is the last twelve chapters of the very famous five volume work by Irenaeus, titled "Against Heresies," which is thought to have been published between the years A.D. 186 and 188. All earlier surviving Christian observations on Bible prophecy were only short comments included in articles that were mainly about other subjects.

Again, the very oldest Christian commentary on scripture (as opposed to a commentary on a scriptural subject) that has survived to the present day is a "Commentary on Daniel," by Hippolytus, which is believed to have been written between the years A.D. 202 and 211.

---

2   Papias is thought to have written his five volume work, titled "Exposition of the Sayings of the Lord," sometime between the years A.D. 95 and 120. Irenaeus called him "a hearer of John." ("Against Heresies, by Irenaeus, Book V, chapter XXXIII, paragraph 4.) But the church of the dark ages did not see fit to preserve any of his writings. We only have ten small fragments from his books that were quoted by writers from before the dark ages.

3   "The Church History," by Eusebius, book 3, chapter 39. From Volume 1 of "The Early Church Fathers: Nicene & Post-Nicent Fathers, second series," edited by Philip Schaff, D.D., LL.D. and Henry Wace, D.D.

Although we only know that Papias was pre-millennial, Both Irenaeus and Hippolytus made many comments that were distinctly Dispensational, as we shall shortly see. The reason for pointing out that these are the very oldest surviving examples of both of these genres is to clearly demonstrate that, contrary to the claims of the naysayers, dispensationalism can be traced back to the very beginnings of Christian teaching in regard to eschatology.

But because they are completely ignorant of all this, many Preterists, Amillennialists, and Covenant Theologians, and even many Premillennialists who hold the doctrine of a post tribulation rapture claim that the church never taught any view except their own during its first millennium or more. We have already noticed that all such claims are inappropriate and vain, for the only thing that is significant is what the Bible says. But in addition to their being unprofitable and vain, all of these claims are completely incorrect.

Before we begin this examination, let it be perfectly clear that this writer considers it wholly unacceptable to attribute any authority whatsoever to these documents, other than their historical value. It is serious bad doctrine to claim that the writings of any man, or of any group of men, are authoritative. Our only true and proper authority is the word of God itself, the Bible.

Also before we begin this study, it seems advisable to note how this book came to be.

In or about 1966, this writer read four commentaries on the book of Ezekiel. When the writers of these four books came to chapters 38 and 39, all four gave the modern identities of all the nations listed in that prophecy as joining together to attack Israel in the last days.

And all four lists were different!

This writer snorted, and said to himself, "Enough of this nonsense. I'm going to find out for myself who they are." At first, he was muttering to himself, "where am I ever going to find this information." But within a few months, this had changed to "where am I ever going to find time to read all these books?" For he had discovered that, only about sixty miles from where he lived at that time, was the fifth largest library in the world. And it had literally hundreds of volumes actually written in ancient times. Each of these very many volumes had the original language and an English translation on facing pages. So it was possible to actually study the works of ancient writers from many nations, without having to learn all the languages involved.

This led to a study that lasted approximately 35 years, during which time this writer studied the most ancient available records of many nations, from Israel, Egypt, Babylon, Persia, Assyria, Armenia, Greece, and Rome, to as far afield as Scandinavia and even China, until he had hard proof from multiple ancient sources of the modern identities of most of the nations mentioned in Bible prophecy. Unfortunately, The Russian language was never reduced to writing until the ninth century. So the oldest available Russian records are medieval, rather than ancient. But these were also studied at length.

But as this writer began to post his findings on the internet, he was met with the inappropriate claim that these ideas could not even possibly be correct, because they were never taught before around 1830 or so.

From his previous studies, he already knew that this was incorrect. But this led him to embark again upon the sea of ancient literature for nearly another ten years, this time studying what many ancient Christian writers had actually taught about Bible prophecy. His main (but not his only) source for this information was the widely circulated set commonly known as "The Early Church Fathers." This is a 38 volume set, divided into three series, titled "Ante-Nicene Fathers," (10 volumes) "Nicene & Post-Nicene Fathers, first series" (14 volumes) and "Nicene & Post-Nicene Fathers, second series." (also 14 volumes) As the average length of these 38 volumes is more than 500 pages, few have actually studied them at length, although many own this remarkable set. Though widely circulated, this extensive documentation of early Christianity is used mainly for reference.

This writer shared his findings with William C. Watson, who strongly encouraged him to reduce his copious notes into the form of a book.[4]

---

4   A note to readers: As ancient texts are quoted in this volume, the most pertinent material has been highlighted using bold text. All emphases made in this way is the writer's and not that of the original author.

INTRODUCTION

As we begin this examination, we need to set in our minds what dispensationalism is. That is, what is its real essence, and what does it entail. If we do not have this firmly in mind, we will not recognize Dispensational doctrine when we see it. So we first need to define Dispensational Doctrine.

Dispensationalism, in its central essence, is simply the doctrine that from time to time, God changes the way He relates to mankind. Opponents of this doctrine often dismiss it as God resorting to "plan B" when "plan A" had failed. But this is not the doctrine at all. It is rather that God is going through a series of demonstrations, which Dispensationalists sometimes call "tests," to prove what He knew from the beginning, that mankind would fail under any conceivable circumstance. This was clearly taught in ancient times, as is noted in chapter 1 of this book.

Dispensationalism springs from a literal interpretation of the explicitly stated prophecies in the Bible, from the assumption that the prophecies actually meant exactly what God said. This, of course, taking into account the usage of well known and widely recognized figures of speech, such as Jesus calling himself both the door and the way (as in "the road,") and also calling himself the bread of life. The importance of this literal interpretation of Bible prophecy was also clearly taught in ancient times, as is traced in chapter 2.

This literal interpretation requires an acceptance of the many prophecies about a future program for the nation of Israel, as meaning exactly what they say. That is, that "Israel" does not mean "the church," and "the land of Israel" does not mean "heaven." Indeed, this literal interpretation of the Biblical prophecies is what led to a revival of the doctrine of dispensationalism in the 1830s. A review of many ancient statements about a prophetic program for the Jews may be found in chapter 3, followed by a review of some that explicitly speak of a future spiritual restoration or revival of Israel in chapter 4.

This literal interpretation of the Biblical prophecies also leads to the understanding that the seventieth week of the famous "seventy weeks" prophecy of Daniel (Daniel 9:24-27) remains to be fulfilled in the future. Again, this was taught, and sometimes in very explicit language, in ancient times, as is shown in chapter 5.

And finally, this led to an understanding that the Lord's return to take his own to himself would take place a significant time before He would return to judge the world for its wickedness. This also was taught in ancient times, as is demonstrated in chapter 6.

But here we need to add a word of caution. None of these writers were actual Dispensationalists, in the modern sense of the word. For many of them also said things that are wholly incompatible with dispensationalism, as it is commonly taught today. Of all of them, Irenaeus and Augustin are the ones whose remarks, as quoted here, sound most like the sayings of modern Dispensationalists. But Irenaeus also taught many of the central elements of Covenant Theology, and Augustin was Amillennial. **The quotations in this book are made solely to demonstrate that the central concepts of dispensationalism extend all the way back to the very beginnings of Christian teachings on the scriptures, and continued to be taught as least as late as the fifth century.**

CHAPTER 1

◆◆◆

Ancient Writers Who Called the Various Ages in which God Dealt With Mankind in Different Ways, "Dispensations"

We find a clear usage of the word dispensation in regard to a period of time in the very oldest Christian commentary on Bible prophecy (of any significant length) that has survived to the present day. This is the famous five volume work by Irenaeus,[5] titled "Against Heresies," which is thought to date from between the years A.D. 186 and 188:

The first statements by Irenaeus we will notice is:

> "... in his own person most clearly **calling Him Lord, who appointed the legal dispensation**. But 'Simeon,' he also says, 'blessed God, and said, Lord, now lettest Thou Thy servant depart in peace; for mine eyes have seen Thy salvation, which Thou hast prepared before the face of all people; a light for the revelation of the Gentiles, and the glory of Thy people Israel.' And 'Anna' also, 'the prophetess,' he says, in like manner glorified God when she saw Christ, 'and spake of Him to all them who were looking for the redemption of Jerusalem.' **Now by all these one God is shown**

---

5   All quotations of Irenaeus in this book are from Volume 1 of "The Early Church Fathers: Ante-Nicene Fathers," edited by Alexander Roberts and James Donaldson, as found in its American edition edited by A. Cleveland Coxe.

forth, revealing to men the new dispensation of liberty, the covenant, through the new advent of His Son." ("Against Heresies," by Irenaeus, book III, chapter X, paragraph 4.)

"As, therefore, He has promised to give very much to those who do now bring forth fruit, according to the gift of His grace, but not according to the changeableness of 'knowledge;' for the Lord remains the same, and the same Father is revealed; thus, therefore, has the one and the same Lord granted, by means of His advent, a greater gift of grace to **those of a later period**, than what He had granted to those under **the Old Testament dispensation**. ("Against Heresies," by Irenaeus, book IV, chapter XI, paragraph 3.)

"Whom these men did therefore preach to the unbelievers as Lord, Him did Christ teach to those who obey Him; and the God who had called those of **the former dispensation**, is the same as He who has received those of **the latter. In other words, He who at first used that law which entails bondage, is also He who did in after times [call His people] by means of adoption.** For God planted the vineyard of the human race when at the first He formed Adam and chose the fathers; then He let it out to husbandmen when He established **the Mosaic dispensation:**" ("Against Heresies," by Irenaeus, book IV, chapter XXXVI, paragraph 2.)

We need to notice in these quotations the opposition of the phrases **"the legal dispensation"** and **"the new dispensation of liberty"** in the first one. Likewise, the similar opposition of the phrases **"the Old Testament Dispensation"** and **"those of a later period"** in the second one. And the opposition of the phrases **"the former dispensation,"** and **"the latter"** in the third one, calling the first age **"the Mosaic dispensation."** So we see that Irenaeus clearly called these various ages "dispensations." And we need to particularly notice the words in the third quotation, "**In other words, He who at first used that law which entails bondage, is also He who did in after times [call His people] by means of adoption.**"

But we need to notice more of the doctrine of Irenaeus:

"Therefore the Son of the Father declares [Him] **from the beginning**, inasmuch as He was with the Father from the beginning, who did also show to the human race prophetic visions, and diversities of gifts, and His own ministrations, and the glory of the Father, **in regular order and connection, at the fitting time** for the benefit [of mankind]. For where there is **a regular succession**, there is also fixedness; and where fixedness, there **suitability to the period**; and where suitability, there also utility. And for this reason did **the Word** become the dispenser of the paternal grace for the benefit of men, for whom He made such great dispensations, revealing God indeed to men, but presenting man to God, and preserving at the same time the invisibility of the Father, lest man should at any time become a despiser of God, and that he should always possess something towards which he might advance; but, on the other hand, **revealing God to men through many dispensations,** lest man, failing away from God altogether, should cease to exist." ("Against Heresies," by Irenaeus, book IV, chapter XX, paragraph 7.)

We need to notice certain key parts of this statement. Irenaeus said that God has "from the beginning" shown "to the human race prophetic visions" "in regular order and connection, at the fitting time," and in "a regular succession," with "suitability to the period," "revealing God to men through many dispensations."

A few chapters later, Irenaeus further said,

"There is one and the same God the Father, and His Word, who has been always present with the human race, by means indeed of various dispensations, and has wrought out many things, and saved from the beginning those who are saved, (for these are they who love God, and follow the Word of God according to the class to which they belong,) and has judged those who are judged, that is, those who forget God, and are blasphemous, and transgressors of His word." ("Against Heresies," by Irenaeus, book IV, chapter XXVIII, paragraph 2.)

We already noticed that Irenaeus said that **"the Word"** was **"revealing God to men through many dispensations,"** and that he said that this was done **"at the fitting time,"** in **"a regular succession,"** with **"suitability to the period."** Now we see that he also said that the Word **"has been always present with the human race,"** and saved various individuals **"according to the class to which they belong."**

These statements were all about past or present dispensations, but Irenaeus also spoke of a future one, saying:

> **"Inasmuch, therefore, as the opinions of certain [orthodox persons] are derived from heretical discourses, they are both ignorant of God's dispensations,** and of the mystery of the resurrection of the just, and of the [earthly] kingdom which is the commencement of incorruption, by means of which kingdom those who shall be worthy are accustomed gradually to partake of the divine nature; and it is necessary to tell them respecting those things, that it behooves the righteous first to receive the promise of the inheritance which God promised to the fathers, and to reign in it, when they rise again to behold God in this creation which is renovated, and that the judgment should take place afterwards." ("Against Heresies," by Irenaeus, book V, chapter XXXII, paragraph 1.)

Here we see that Irenaeus taught that ignorance **"of Gods dispensations"** kept men from understanding the Biblical prophecies of a future age on this earth.

All this is the very central essence of dispensationalism. For although it involves many other details, the central core of the doctrine of dispensationalism is that in different ages God deals with mankind in different ways. Indeed, a difference in dealing is what the very word itself implies, for the Greek word translated **"dispensation"** in Ephesians 1:10, from which this doctrine derives its name, is οἰκονομίαν (word number 3622 in Strong's Greek Dictionary.) This Greek word literally translates as "administration," which is the central essence of the doctrine.

That is, Dispensationalism, at its very core, is the doctrine that, although the basic ways of God never change, He administers his relationship with mankind in different ways in different ages. This is precisely what Irenaeus was saying in the statements quoted above.

But Irenaeus did not just speak of a single past age, he also spoke of four covenants of God (three past covenants and the present one) saying:

> "For this reason were four principal covenants given to the human race: one, prior to the deluge, under Adam; the second, that after the deluge, under Noah; the third, the giving of the law, under Moses; the fourth, that which renovates man, and sums up all things in itself by means of the Gospel arising and bearing men upon its wings into the heavenly kingdom." ("Against Heresies," by Irenaeus, book III, chapter XI, paragraph 8.)

And lest anyone imagine that here, Irenaeus was actually teaching Covenant Theology, this statement needs to be considered in the light of all this writer said about the various dispensations.

Irenaeus insisted that this doctrine of the dispensations was what the church had always taught, saying,

> "The Church, though dispersed through our the whole world, even to the ends of the earth, has received from the apostles and their disciples this faith: [She believes] in one God, the Father Almighty, Maker of heaven, and earth, and the sea, and all things

that are in them; and in one Christ Jesus, the Son of God, who became incarnate for our salvation; and in the Holy Spirit, who proclaimed through the prophets the dispensations of God, and the advents..." ("Against Heresies," by Irenaeus, book I, chapter X, paragraph 1.)

He said again:

"But [it has, on the other hand, been shown], that the preaching of the Church is everywhere consistent, and continues in an even course, and receives testimony from the prophets, the apostles, and all the disciples—as I have proved—through [those in] the beginning, the middle, and the end, and through the entire dispensation of God, and that well-grounded system which tends to man's salvation, namely, our faith; which, having been received from the Church, we do preserve, and which always, by the Spirit of God, renewing its youth, as if it were some precious deposit in an excellent vessel, causes the vessel itself containing it to renew its youth also. For this gift of God has been entrusted to the Church, as breath was to the first created man, for this purpose, that all the members receiving it may be vivified; and the [means of] communion with Christ has been distributed throughout it, that is, the Holy Spirit, the earnest of incorruption, the means of confirming our faith, and the ladder of ascent to God." ("Against Heresies," by Irenaeus, book III, chapter XXIV, paragraph 1.)

And:

"But that both the apostles and their disciples thus taught as the Church preaches, and thus teaching were perfected, wherefore also they were called away to that which is perfect—Stephen, teaching these truths, when he was yet on earth, saw the glory of God, and Jesus on His right hand, and exclaimed, 'Behold, I see the heavens opened, and the Son of man standing on the right hand of God.' (Acts 7:56) These words he said, and was stoned; and thus did he fulfil the perfect doctrine, copying in every respect the Leader of martyrdom, and praying for those who were slaying him, in these words: 'Lord, lay not this sin to their charge.' **Thus were they perfected who knew one and the same God, who from beginning to end was present with mankind in the various dispensations; as the prophet Hosea declares: 'I have filled up visions, and used similitudes by the hands of the prophets.' ** " ("Against Heresies," by Irenaeus, book III, chapter XII, paragraph 13.)

Another widely circulated early document which clearly used the word "dispensation" to describe an age, was "The Shepherd of Hermas," also called "The Pastor of Hermas," which is thought to be even older than the famous work by Irenaeus, although its treatment of prophecy is very short. It is thought have been written around A.D. 160, although some date it as early as A.D. 100. This document says:

> "'First of all, sir,' I said, 'explain this to me: What is the meaning of the rock and the gate?' 'This rock,' he answered, 'and this gate are the Son of God.' 'How, sir?' I said; 'the rock is old, and the gate is new.' 'Listen,' he said, 'and understand, O ignorant man. The Son of God is older than all His creatures, so that He was a fellow-councillor with the Father in His work of creation: for this reason is He old.' 'And why is the gate new, sir?' I said. 'Because,' he answered, **'He became manifest in the last days of the dispensation:** for this reason the gate was made new, that they who are to be saved by it might enter into the kingdom of God.'" [6]

This writer was clearly using the word "dispensation" for a period of time, as shown by the words **"He became manifest in the last days of the dispensation."**

---

6 "The Pastor" by Hermas," Book Third-Similitudes, Similitude Ninth, chapter 12. From Volume 2 of "The Early Church Fathers: Ante-Nicene Fathers," edited by Alexander Roberts, D.D. and James Donaldson, LL.D. as revised by A. Cleveland Coxe, D.D.

We next come to Tertullian,[7] who is believed to have written his famous works against Marcion between A.D. 207 and 208. He is often called "the father of Latin Christianity. Tertullian said:

> "I do allow that **one order did run its course in the old dispensation under the Creator, and that another is on its way in the new under Christ.** I do not deny that there is a difference in the language of their documents, in their precepts of virtue, and in their teachings of the law; but yet all this diversity is consistent with one and the same God, even Him by whom it was arranged and also foretold... But why enlarge, when the Creator by the same prophet foretells the renovation more manifestly and clearly than the light itself? 'Remember not the former things, neither consider the things of old' (the old things have passed away, and new things are arising). 'Behold, I will do new things, which shall now spring forth.' So by Jeremiah: 'Break up for yourselves new pastures, and sow not among thorns, and circumcise yourselves in the foreskin of your heart.' **And in another passage: 'Behold, the days come, saith the Lord, that I will make a new covenant with the house of Jacob, and with the house of Judah; not according to the covenant that I made with their fathers in the day when I arrested their dispensation, in order to bring them out of the land of Egypt.' He thus shows that the ancient covenant is temporary only, when He indicates its change; also when He promises that it shall be followed by an eternal one.** For by Isaiah He says: 'Hear me, and ye shall live; and I will make an everlasting covenant with you,' adding 'the sure mercies of David,' in order that He might show that covenant was to run its course in Christ... **Forasmuch then as he said, that from the Creator there would come other laws, and other words, and new dispensations of covenants, indicating also that the very sacrifices were to receive higher offices, and that amongst all nations, by Malachi when he says: 'I have no pleasure in you, saith the Lord, neither will I accept**

---

7   All quotations of Tertullian in this book are from volume 3 of Ante-Nicene Fathers," edited by Alexander Roberts, D.D. and James Donaldson, LL.D. as revised by A. Cleveland Coxe, D.D.

your sacrifices at your hands. For from the rising of the sun, even unto the going down of the same, my name shall be great among the Gentiles; and in every place a sacrifice is offered unto my name, even a pure offering' —meaning simple prayer from a pure conscience,—it is of necessity that every change which comes as the result of innovation, introduces a diversity in those things of which the change is made, from which diversity arises also a contrariety." ("Against Marcion," by Tertullian, Book 4, chapter 1.)

Here, in the words, "one order did run its course in the old dispensation under the Creator, and that another is on its way in the new under Christ," Tertullian was clearly using the word "dispensation" to describe two different periods of time.

But Tertullian further said:

"But, you object, the world to come bears the character of a different dispensation, even an eternal one; and therefore, you maintain, that the non-eternal substance of this life is incapable of possessing a state of such different features. **This would be true enough, if man were made for the future dispensation, and not the dispensation for man."** ("On the Resurrection of the Flesh," by Tertullian, Chap. LIX, titled "Our Flesh in the Resurrection Capable, Without Losing Its Essential Identity, of Bearing the Changed Conditions of Eternal Life, or of Death Eternal." from book VI of "The Writings of Tertullian Part Second.)

This is of note in that it shows that both sides in this debate called "**the world to come**" "**a different dispensation.**"

Again, Cyprian, who is considered the pre-eminent Latin writer of Western Christianity up to the times of Jerome and Augustine, wrote at some time, as it is thought, between 248 and 258. Cyprian said:

"And indeed, as you have asked, so has this discourse been arranged by me; and this treatise has been ordered in an abridged compendium, so that I should not scatter what was written in too diffuse an abundance, but, as far as my poor memory suggested, might collect all that was necessary in selected and connected heads, under which I may seem, not so much to have treated the subject, as to have afforded material for others to treat it...

"9. That the former law, which was given by Moses, was about to cease.

10. That a new law was to be given.

11. That another dispensation and a new covenant was to be given..." [8]

And even as late as the turn of the fifth century, this concept had not yet been lost. Around that time, Jerome and Augustin exchanged a series of letters from which the following quotations were extracted, in which they both repeatedly spoke of the various ages in which God related to mankind in different ways, calling them "dispensations."

"Instead of the grace of the law which has passed away, we have received the grace of the gospel which is abiding; and instead of the shadows and types of the old dispensation, the truth has come by Jesus Christ. Jeremiah also prophesied thus in God's name: "Behold, the days come, saith the Lord, that I will make a new covenant with the house of Israel, and with the house of Judah; not according to the covenant which I made with their Fathers," in the day that I took them by the hand, to bring them out of the land of Egypt." Observe what the prophet says, not to Gentiles, who had not been partakers in any former covenant, but to the Jewish nation. He who has given them the law by Moses, promises in place of it the new covenant of the gospel, that they might no longer live in the oldness of the letter, but in the newness of the spirit." ("Letters of St. Augustin," translated by J. G. Cunningham, M.A.,

---

8   "Three Books of Testimonies Against the Jews," by Cyprian, Treatise XII of The Treatises of Cyprian. From volume 5 of "Ante-Nicene Fathers," edited by Alexander Roberts, D.D. and James Donaldson, LL.D. as revised by A. Cleveland Coxe, D.D.

Second Division, Letter 75 [A.D. 404] Jerome's answer to Augustin's letters 28. 40, and 71, by Jerome, chapter 4, paragraph 14.⁹)

"In this, moreover, he [Paul] differed from them, that after the passion and resurrection of Christ, in whom had been given and made manifest the mystery of grace, according to the order of Melchizedek, **they still considered it binding on them to celebrate, not out of mere reverence for old customs, but as necessary to salvation, the sacraments of the old dispensation; which were indeed at one time necessary, else had it been unprofitable and vain for the Maccabees to suffer martyrdom as they did for their adherence to them.**" ("Letters of St. Augustin," translated by J. G. Cunningham, M.A., Second Division, Letter 75 [A.D. 404] Jerome's answer to Augustin's letters 28. 40, and 71, by Jerome, chapter 4, paragraph 15.)

"As to Paul's circumcising of Timothy, performing a vow at Cenchrea, and undertaking on the suggestion of James at Jerusalem to share the performance of the appointed rites with some who had made a vow, **it is manifest that Paul's design in these things was not to give to others the impression that he thought that by these observances salvation is given under the Christian dispensation, but to prevent men from believing that he condemned as no better than heathen idolatrous worship, those rites which God had appointed in the former dispensation as suitable to it, and as shadows of things to come.**" ("Letters of St. Augustin," by Augustin, translated by J. G. Cunningham, M.A., Second Division, Letter 82 [A.D. 405] to Jerome, reply to letters 72, 75, and 81, chapter 2, paragraph 8.)

"For the men who had brought this reproach against Paul were not those who understood the right spirit in which observance

9   All the letters to or from Augustin in this book are from "Nicene and Post-Nicene Fathers," First Series, volume 1, Edited by Philip Schaff, D.D., LL.D.

of these ceremonies should be practised under the Christian dispensation by believing Jews, — **namely, as a way of declaring the divine authority of these rites, and their holy use in the prophetic dispensation, and not as a means of obtaining salvation,** which was to them already revealed in Christ and ministered by baptism. On the contrary, the men who had spread abroad this report against the apostle were those who would have these rites observed, as if without their observance there could be no salvation to those who believed the gospel. For these false teachers had found him to be a most zealous preacher of free grace, and a most decided opponent of their views, teaching as he did that men are not justified by these things, but by the grace of Jesus Christ, which these ceremonies of the law were appointed to foreshadow." ("Letters of St. Augustin," by Augustin, translated by J. G. Cunningham, M.A., Second Division, Letter 82 [A.D. 405] to Jerome, reply to letters 72, 75, and 81, chapter 2, paragraph 9.)

"And I now, as speaking in the sight of God, beseech you by the law of charity to believe me when I say with my whole heart, that **it never was my opinion that in our time, Jews who become Christians were either required or at liberty to observe in any manner, or from any motive whatever, the ceremonies of the ancient dispensation;** although I have always held, in regard to the Apostle Paul, the opinion which you call in question, from the time that I became acquainted with his writings." ("Letters of St. Augustin," by Augustin, translated by J. G. Cunningham, M.A., Second Division, Letter 82 [A.D. 405] to Jerome, reply to letters 72, 75, and 81, chapter 2, paragraph 17.)

"When, therefore, he did not refuse to practise some of these Old Testament observances, he was not led by his compassion for Jews to feign this conformity, but unquestionably was acting sincerely; **and by this course of action declaring his respect for those things which in the former dispensation had been for a**

time enjoined by God, he distinguished between them and the impious rites of heathenism." ("Letters of St. Augustin," by Augustin, translated by J. G. Cunningham, M.A., Second Division, Letter 82 [A.D. 405] to Jerome, reply to letters 72, 75, and 81, chapter 3, paragraph 28.)

In addition to the letters in this exchange with Jerome, Augustin also penned many other letters in which he said similar things, as follows:

"Had I been a Jew in the time of that ancient people, when there was nothing better that I could be, I would undoubtedly have received circumcision. That **"seal of the righteousness which is by faith" was of so great importance in that dispensation before it was abrogated by the Lord's coming,** that the angel would have strangled the infant- child of Moses, had not the child's mother, seizing a stone, circumcised the child, and by this sacrament averted impending death. This sacrament also arrested the waters of the Jordan, and made them flow back towards their source. This sacrament the Lord Himself received in infancy, although He abrogated it when He was crucified. **For these signs of spiritual blessings were not condemned, but gave place to others which were more suitable to the later dispensation. For as circumcision was abolished by the first coming of the Lord, so baptism shall be abolished by His second coming.** For as now, since the liberty of faith has come, and the yoke of bondage has been removed, no Christian receives circumcision in the flesh; so then, when the just are reigning with the Lord, and the wicked have been condemned, no one shall be baptized, but the reality which both ordinances prefigure—namely, circumcision of the heart and cleansing of the conscience—shall be eternally abiding. **If, therefore, I had been a Jew in the time of the former dispensation, and there had come to me a Samaritan who was willing to become a Jew,** abandoning the error which the Lord Himself condemned when He said, "Ye worship ye know not what; we know what we worship, for salvation is of the Jews;" —if, I say, a Samaritan whom Samaritans had circumcised had expressed his willingness to become a Jew, there would have been no scope for the boldness which would have insisted on the repetition of the rite; and instead of this, we would have been compelled to approve of that which God had commanded, although it had been done by heretics." ("Letters of St. Augustin," by Augustin, translated by J. G. Cunningham, M.A., First Division, Letter 23, [A.D. 392] To Maximin, paragraph 4.)

"After awakening their attention by bringing forward the subject of immoderate indulgence in wine, I myself also read this chapter, and added to it an argument to prove with how much greater anger and vehemence our Lord would cast forth drunken revels, which are everywhere disgraceful, from that temple from which He thus drove out merchandise lawful elsewhere, especially when the things sold **were those required for the sacrifices appointed in that dispensation**; and I asked them whether they regarded a place occupied by men selling what was necessary, or one used by men drinking to excess, as bearing the greater resemblance to a den of thieves." ("Letters of St. Augustin," by Augustin, translated by J. G. Cunningham, M.A., First Division, Letter 29 [A.D. 395] to Alypius, paragraph 3.)

"I asked further, with the deepest sorrow, how it was that, although Moses the servant of God broke both the tables of stone because of these rulers of Israel, I could not break the hearts of those who, **though men of the New Testament dispensation,** were desiring in their celebration of saints' days to repeat often the public perpetration of excesses of which the people of the Old Testament economy were guilty only once, and that in an act of idolatry." ("Letters of St. Augustin," by Augustin, translated by J. G. Cunningham, M.A., First Division, Letter 29 [A.D. 395] to Alypius, paragraph 4.)

"But God did not lay down a rule concerning fasting or eating on the seventh day of the week, either at the time of His hallowing that day because in it He rested from His works, or afterwards, when He gave precepts to the Hebrew nation concerning the observance of that day. The only thing enjoined on man there is, that he abstain from doing work himself, or requiring it from his servants. **And the people of the former dispensation, accepting this rest as a shadow of things to come, obeyed the command by such abstinence from work as we now see practised by the Jews; not, as some suppose, through their being carnal, and misunderstanding what the Christians rightly understand.** Nor do we understand this law better than the prophets, who, at the time when this was still binding, observed such rest on the Sabbath as the Jews believe ought to be observed to this day." ("Letters of St. Augustin," by Augustin, translated by J. G. Cunningham, M.A., Second Division, Letter 36 [A.D. 396] to Casulanus, chapter 3, paragraph 5.)

"Let him therefore consider whether it might not with more reason be said in reply to him, that the Lord desired to have these two things, the plucking of the ears of corn and the taking of food, done in the same day by His disciples, for this reason, that the former action might confute those who would prohibit all work on the seventh day, and the latter action confute those who would enjoin fasting on the seventh day; **since by the former action He taught that the rest from labour was now, through the change in the dispensation, an act of superstition; and by the latter He intimated His will, that under both dispensations the matter of fasting or not was left to every man's choice.**" ("Letters of St. Augustin," by Augustin, translated by J. G. Cunningham, M.A., Second Division, Letter 36 [A.D. 396] to Casulanus, chapter 3, paragraph 6.)

"I know that I have omitted many examples: let those who are willing and able read the divine records for themselves: they will find that all the holy servants and friends of God have always had to bear with some among their own people, with whom, nevertheless, **they partook in the sacraments of that dispensation,** and in so doing not only were not defiled by them, but were to be commended for their tolerant spirit, 'endeavouring to keep,' as the apostle says, 'the unity of the Spirit in the bond of peace.'" ("Letters of St. Augustin," by Augustin, translated by J. G. Cunningham, M.A., Second Division, Letter 43 [A.D. 397] to Glorianus, Eleusius, etc., chapter 8, paragraph 23.)

"You are doubtless aware that in the Jewish dispensation the sin of idolatry was committed by the people, and once the book of the prophet of God was burned by a defiant king; the punishment of the sin of schism would not have been more severe than that with which these two were visited, had not the guilt of it been greater." ("Letters of St. Augustin," by Augustin, translated by J. G. Cunningham, M.A., Second Division, Letter 51 [A.D. 399 or 400] to Crispinus, paragraph 1.)

"I desire you therefore, in the first place, to hold fast this as the fundamental principle in the present discussion, that our Lord Jesus Christ has appointed to us a "light yoke" and an "easy burden," as He declares in the Gospel: **in accordance with which He has bound His people under the new dispensation together in fellowship by sacraments, which are in number very few, in observance most easy, and in significance most excellent,** as baptism solemnized in the name of the Trinity, the communion of His body and blood, and such other things as are prescribed in the canonical Scriptures, with the exception of those enactments which were a yoke of bondage to God's ancient people, suited to their state of heart and to the times of the prophets, and which are found in the five books of Moses." ("Letters of St. Augustin," by Augustin, translated by J. G. Cunningham, M.A., Second Division, Letter 54 [A.D. 400] to Januarius, chapter 1, paragraph 1.)

"... we borrow in our discourses manifold figures; and in the celebration of sacraments, the very few things which the comparative liberty of the Christian dispensation has prescribed, such as water, bread, wine, and oil. Under the bondage, however, of the ancient dispensation many rites were prescribed, which are made known to us only for our instruction as to their meaning." ("Letters of St. Augustin," by Augustin, translated by J. G. Cunningham, M.A., Second Division, Letter 55 [A.D. 400] to Januarius, chapter 7, paragraph 13.)

"For a change, not of the God, who is worshipped, nor of the religion itself, but of sacrifices and of sacraments, would seem to be proclaimed without warrant now, if it had not been foretold in the earlier dispensation. For just as when the same man brings to God in the morning one kind of offering, and in the evening another, according to the time of day, he does not thereby change either his God or his religion, any more than he changes the nature of a salutation who uses one form of salutation in the morning and another in the evening: so, in the complete cycle of the ages, when one kind of offering is known to have been made by the ancient saints, and another is presented by the saints in our time, this only shows that these sacred mysteries are celebrated not according to human presumption, but by divine authority, in the manner best adapted to the times. There is here no change either in the Deity or in the religion." ("Letters of St. Augustin," by Augustin, translated by J. G. Cunningham, M.A., Second Division, Letter 102 [A.D. 409] to Deogratias, paragraph 21.)

"Wherefore the shadow of that gourd over his head prefigured the promises of the Old Testament, or rather the privileges already enjoyed in it, in which there was, as the apostle says, "a shadow of things to come," furnishing, as it were, a refuge from the heat of temporal calamities in the land of promise. Moreover, in that morning-worm, which by its gnawing tooth made the gourd wither away, Christ Himself is again prefigured, forasmuch as, by the publication of the gospel from His mouth, all those things which flourished among the Israelites for a time, or with a shadowy symbolical meaning in that earlier dispensation, are now deprived of their significance, and have withered away." ("Letters of St. Augustin," by Augustin, translated by J. G. Cunningham, M.A., Second Division, Letter 102 [A.D. 409] to Deogratias, paragraph 35.)

"For unto those men who incessantly reproach the Christian faith, impiously saying that the human race did not suffer such grievous calamities before the Christian doctrine was promulgated throughout the world, it is easy to find a reply in the Lord's own words in the gospel, 'That servant which knew not his lord's will, and did commit things worthy of stripes, shall be beaten with few stripes; but the servant which knew his lord's will, and prepared not himself, neither did according to his will, shall be beaten with many stripes.' **What is there to excite surprise, if, in the Christian dispensation, the world, like that servant, knowing the will of the Lord, and refusing to do it, is beaten with many stripes?**" ("Letters of St. Augustin," by Augustin, translated by J. G. Cunningham, M.A., Second Division, Letter 111 [November, A.D. 409] to Victorianus, paragraph 2.)

"The divine institution of sacrifice was suitable in the former dispensation, but is not suitable now. For the change suitable to the present age has been enjoined by God, who knows infinitely better than man what is fitting for every age, and who is, whether He give or add, abolish or curtail, increase or diminish, the unchangeable Governor as He is the unchangeable Creator of mutable things, ordering all events in His providence until the beauty of the completed course of time, the component parts of which are the dispensations adapted to each successive age, shall be finished, like the grand melody of some ineffably wise master of song, and those pass into the

eternal immediate contemplation of God who here, though it is a time of faith, not of sight, are acceptably worshipping Him." ("Letters of Augustin, Third Division, Letter 138 - to Marcellinus," by Augustin, paragraph 5.)

This, again, is the very essence of dispensationalism. For it teaches that, although God is unchangeable, he deals with mankind in different ways in different ages.

Further down in the same letter, Augustin went on to say,

"It would, however, take too long to discuss with adequate fulness the differences between the symbolical actions of former and present times, which, because of their pertaining to divine things, are called sacraments. For as the man is not fickle who does one thing in the morning and another in the evening, one thing this month and another in the next, one thing this year and another next year, so there is no variableness with God, though in the former period of the world's history He enjoined one kind of offerings, and in the latter period another, therein ordering the symbolical actions pertaining to the blessed doctrine of true religion in harmony with the changes of successive epochs without any change in Himself. **For in order to let those whom these things perplex understand that the change was already in the divine counsel, and that, when the new ordinances were appointed, it was not because the old had suddenly lost the divine approbation through inconstancy in His will, but that this had been already fixed and determined by the wisdom of that God to whom, in reference to much greater changes, these words are spoken in Scripture: Thou shalt change them, and they shall be changed; but Thou art the same,**"—it is necessary to convince them that this exchange of the sacraments of the Old Testament for those of the New had been predicted by the voices of the prophets.**" ("Letters of Augustin, Third Division, Letter 138 - to Marcellinus," by Augustin, paragraph 7.)

It is a major tenet of dispensationalism, that the changes in the ways God deals with humanity were all part of His basic plan from the very beginning. Opponents of dispensationalism often mock this as imagining that the church is God's "plan B." But dispensationalism actually teaches that these changes had been a part of God's overall plan from the very beginning. So in these comments, Augustin was defending Dispensational concepts in the same way that modern Dispensationalists defend them.

We now move from the letters of Augustin to his many other writings.

"Now, since God by the words, 'Adam, where art thou?' pointed to the death of the soul, which results when He abandons it, and since in the words, 'Earth thou art, and unto earth shalt thou return,' He signified the death of the body, which results when the soul departs from it, **we are led, therefore, to believe that He said nothing of the second death, wishing it to be kept hidden, and reserving it for the New Testament dispensation, in which it is most plainly revealed.**" [10]

"**Now, certainly, it is written most clearly in the Epistle to the Hebrews, when the dispensation of the New Testament was to be distinguished from the dispensation of the Old, according to the fitness of ages and of times, that not only those visible things, but also the word itself, was wrought by angels.** For it is said thus: 'But to which of the angels said He at any time, Sit on my right hand, until I make thine enemies thy footstool? Are they not all ministering spirits, sent forth to minister for them who shall be heirs of salvation?'" [11]

---

10 "The City of God," by Augustin, translated by Marcus Dods, D.D., book XIII, chapter 23. From "Nicene and Post-Nicene Fathers," First Series, volume 2, Edited by Philip Schaff, D.D., LL.D.

11 "On The Trinity," by Augustin, translated by Arthur West Haddan, B.D., revised by William G. T. Shedd, D.D., book III, chapter 11, paragraph 22. From "Nicene and Post-Nicene Fathers," First Series, volume 3, Edited by Philip Schaff, D.D., LL.D.

"Five ages of the world, accordingly, having been now completed (there has entered the sixth). Of these ages the first is from the beginning of the human race, that is, from Adam, who was the first man that was made, down to Noah, who constructed the ark at the time of the flood. **Then the second extends from that period on to Abraham,** who was called the father indeed of all nations which should follow the example of his faith, but who at the same time in the way of natural descent from his own flesh was the father of the destined people of the Jews; which people, previous to the entrance of the Gentiles into the Christian faith, was the one people among all the nations of all lands that worshipped the one true God: from which people also Christ the Saviour was decreed to come according to the flesh. For these turning-points of those two ages occupy an eminent place in the ancient books. On the other hand, those of the other three ages are also declared in the Gospel, where the descent of the Lord Jesus Christ according to the flesh is likewise mentioned. For **the third age extends from Abraham on to David the king; the fourth from David on to that captivity whereby the people of God passed over into Babylonia; and the fifth from that transmigration down to the advent of our Lord Jesus Christ. With His coming the sixth age has entered on its process;** so that now the spiritual grace, which in previous times was known to a few patriarchs and prophets, may be made manifest to all nations; to the intent that no man should worship God but freely, fondly desiring of Him not the visible rewards of His services and the happiness of this present life, but that eternal life alone in which he is to enjoy God Himself: in order that in this sixth age the mind of man may be renewed after the image of God, even as on the sixth day man was made after the image of God." [12]

Here, again, Augustin was teaching the very essence of dispensationalism, although he did not use that word. And, although he divided them

---

12 "On the Catechising of the Uninstructed," by Augustin, translated by S. D. F. Salmond, D.D., chapter 22, paragraph 39. From "Nicene and Post-Nicene Fathers," First Series, volume 3, Edited by Philip Schaff, D.D., LL.D.

differently, he had the same number of past and present ages as is most commonly taught by modern Dispensationalists.

"Thus, then, showing forth the New Testament of our everlasting inheritance, wherein man was to be renewed by the grace of God and lead a new life, that is, a spiritual life; **and with the view of exhibiting the first one as an old dispensation, wherein a carnal people acting out the old man (with the exception of a few patriarchs and prophets, who had understanding, and some hidden saints), and leading a carnal life, desiderated carnal rewards at the hands of the Lord God**, and received in that fashion but the figures of spiritual blessings..." [13]

"From not making this distinction, the Manichæans, and all who find fault with the writings of the Old Testament, not seeing that whatever observance God appointed for the former dispensation was a shadow of future things, because these observances are now discontinued, condemn them, though no doubt what is unsuitable now was perfectly suitable then as prefiguring the things now revealed." [14]

"The saying of the apostle, that 'to the pure all things are pure,' and that 'every creature of God is good,' is not opposed to the prohibitions of the Old Testament; and the explanation, if they can understand it, is this. **The apostle speaks of the natures of the things, while the Old Testament calls some animals unclean, not in their nature, but symbolically, on account of the prefigurative character of that dispensation.** For instance, a pig and a lamb are both clean in their nature, for every creature of God is good; but symbolically, a lamb is clean, and a pig unclean." [15]

---

13   Ibid, paragraph 40.

14   "Reply to Faustus the Manichæan," by Augustin, translated by Richard Stothert, M.A., [A.D. 400] book VI, paragraph 2. From "Nicene and Post-Nicene Fathers," First Series, volume 4, Edited by Philip Schaff, D.D., LL.D.

15   Ibid, book VI, paragraph 7.

"The elders who pleased God kept their own order by their obedience, in observing, according to God's arrangement, what was appointed as suitable to certain times. So, although all animals intended for food are by nature clean, they abstained from some which had then a symbolical uncleanness, in preparation for the future revelation of the things signified. **And so with regard to unleavened bread and all such things, in which the apostle says there was a shadow of future things, neglect of their observance under the old dispensation, when this observance was enjoined, and was employed to prefigure what was afterwards to be revealed, would have been as criminal, as it would now be foolish in us, after the light of the New Testament has arisen, to think that these predictive observances could be of any use to us.**" [16]

"This love, by which also the righteousness of the law can be fulfilled was bestowed in its significance by Christ in His coming, through the spirit which He sent according to His promise; and therefore He said, 'I came not to destroy the law, but to fulfill it.' **This is the New Testament in which the promise of the kingdom of heaven is made to this love; which was typified in the Old Testament, suitably to the times of that dispensation.** So Christ says again; 'A new commandment I give unto you, that ye love one another.'" [17]

"**Those things in the Old Testament which we do not observe we hold to have been suitable appointments for the time and the people of that dispensation, besides being symbolical to us of truths in which they have still a spiritual use, though the outward observance is abolished;** and this opinion is proved to be the doctrine of the apostolic writings." [18]

---

16   Ibid, book VI, paragraph 9.
17   Ibid, book XIX, paragraph 27.
18   Ibid, book XXII, paragraph 8.

"At whatever time, therefore, men have begun to be of such a nature in this life, that, **although they have partaken of such divine sacraments as were appointed for the dispensation under which they lived,** they yet savor of carnal things, and hope for and desire carnal things from God, whether in this life or afterwards, they are yet carnal." ("On Baptism, Against the Donatists," by Augustin, translated by J. R. King, M.A., [circa 400] book1, chapter 15, paragraph 24. From "Nicene and Post-Nicene Fathers," First Series, volume 4, Edited by Philip Schaff, D.D., LL.D.)

"But since they were ordered to be baptized by the authority of an apostle, it is sufficiently made manifest that that water with which John baptized had no reference to the baptism of Christ, **but belonged to another dispensation suited to the exigencies of the times."** [19]

"In the Old Testament, indeed, that was hidden (conformably to the perfectly just dispensation of the times) which is now revealed in the New Testament." [20]

"This grace hid itself under a veil in the Old Testament, but it has been revealed in the New Testament **according to the most perfectly ordered dispensation of the ages,** forasmuch as God knew how to dispose all things." [21]

"These pertain to the new testament, are the children of promise, and are regenerated by God the Father and a free mother.

---

19 "Answer to Petilian, the Donatist" by Augustin, translated by J. R. King, M.A., [circa 400] book II, chapter 32, paragraph 75. From "Nicene and Post-Nicene Fathers," First Series, volume 4, Edited by Philip Schaff, D.D., LL.D.

20 "A Treatise on the Merits and Forgiveness of Sins, and on the Baptism of Infants," by Augustin, [A.D. 412] book I, chapter 13. From "Nicene and Post-Nicene Fathers," First Series, volume 5, Edited by Philip Schaff, D.D., LL.D.

21 "A Treatise on the Spirit and the Letter," by Augustin, [A.D. 412] chapter 27. From "Nicene and Post-Nicene Fathers," First Series, volume 5, Edited by Philip Schaff, D.D., LL.D.

Of this kind were all the righteous men of old, and Moses himself, the minister of the old testament, the heir of the new, — because of the faith whereby we live, of one and the same they lived, believing the incarnation, passion, and resurrection of Christ as future, which we believe as already accomplished, — **even until John the Baptist himself, as it were a certain limit of the old dispensation, who, signifying that the Mediator Himself would come,** not with any shadow of the future or allegorical intimation, or with any prophetical announcement, but pointing Him out with his finger, said: 'Behold the Lamb of God; behold Him who taketh away the sin of the world.'" [22]

"On this point, also, in reference to what has been said above, I think we may get a still better understanding of the words, 'A little while, and ye shall no more see me: and again a little while, and ye shall see me.' **For the whole of that space over which the present dispensation extends, is but a little while; and hence this same evangelist says in his epistle, 'It is the last hour.'**" [23]

We now move on to Augustin's contemporary, John Crysostem, which means "Golden Tongued John."

"Fearful, indeed, and of most awful import, were **the things which were used before the dispensation of grace,** as the bells, the pomegranates, the stones on the breastplate and on the ephod, the girdle, the mitre, the long robe, the plate of gold, the holy of holies, the deep silence within. But if any one should examine **the things which belong to the dispensation of grace,** he will find that, small as they are, yet are they fearful and full of awe..." [24]

---

22 "A Treatise Against Two Letters of the Pelagians," by Augustin, [circa 420] book III, chapter 11. From "Nicene and Post-Nicene Fathers," First Series, volume 5, Edited by Philip Schaff, D.D., LL.D.

23 "Tractates on the Gospel According to St. John" by Augustin, translated by John Gibb, D.D., Tractate CI, Chapter XVI. 16-23, paragraph 6. From "Nicene and Post-Nicene Fathers," First Series, volume 7, Edited by Philip Schaff, D.D., LL.D.

24 "Treatise Concerning the Christian Priesthood," by John Chrysostom, translated by W. R. E. Ste-

"For this body, even if it reaches a very high standard of beauty is nevertheless perishable; but the bodies of those who have been well pleasing to God, will be invested with such glory as these eyes cannot even look upon. **And God has furnished us with certain tokens, and obscure indications of these things both in the Old and in the New Dispensation.** For in the former the face of Moses shone with such glory as to be intolerable to the eyes of the Israelites, and in the New the face of Christ shone far more brilliantly than his." [25]

"For I can prove to you that this which seems to you onerous was accomplished **under the Old Dispensation** when the manifestation of spiritual wisdom was not so great as it is now." [26]

"Knowing these things, then, brethren, and gathering up what has been now advanced, as well as what has been said before; let us at last desist from this evil custom, yea, I pray and beseech you all! **For if in the old dispensation, when the Jews had not the strictest moral wisdom required of them, but much condescension was extended to them, such wrath was the effect of one oath;** such capture and captivity; what punishment is it likely that those who swear should now be subjected to, after an express law forbidding the practice, and so large an addition of precepts." [27]

"Seest thou how again He connects the old dispensation with the new, signifying that those of old not only knew the things

phens, M.A., book III, paragraph 4. From "Nicene and Post-Nicene Fathers," First Series, volume 9, Edited by Philip Schaff, D.D., LL.D.

25 "Letter to a Young Widow," by John Chrysostom, translated by W. R. E. Stephens, M.A. From "Nicene and Post-Nicene Fathers," First Series, volume 9, Edited by Philip Schaff, D.D., LL.D.

26 "Homily to Those Who Had Not Attended the Assembly," by John Chrysostom, translated by W. R. E. Stephens, M.A., book III, paragraph 4. From "Nicene and Post-Nicene Fathers," First Series, volume 9, Edited by Philip Schaff, D.D., LL.D.

27 "The Homilies on the Statues to the People of Antioch," by John Chrysostom, translated by W. R. E. Stephens, M.A., Homily XIX, paragraph 12. From "Nicene and Post-Nicene Fathers," First Series, volume 9, Edited by Philip Schaff, D.D., LL.D.

to come but also greatly desired them? But had they pertained to some strange and opposing God, they would never have desired them." [28]

"And yet what is equal to virginity, which **not even in the new dispensation hath come under the compulsion of law,** on account of its high excellence? but nevertheless it is cast out, when it hath not almsgiving." [29]

So in conclusion, we see that this practice of calling the various ages in which God dealt with mankind in different ways, "Dispensations," was used in the very oldest writings connected with this subject which have survived to the present day. And that it continued to be used at least into the fifth century.

As the naysayers stress, it was around the year 1830 that the doctrine of dispensationalism began spreading widely, first in England and on the Continent of Europe, and later in the United States. The main leader of the group that led this effort was J.N. Darby, who is erroneously said to have originated the concept. We know from his own writings that he had studied the "Church Fathers," as they are called. So is it any wonder that when he began to write on this subject, he used the same word they used, in the same way they used it, like them calling the various ages in which God related to mankind in different ways, "Dispensations?"

---

28 "Homilies on the Gospel of Saint Matthew," by John Crysostom, Homily XLV, Matt 13:10, 11, paragraph 2. From "Nicene and Post-Nicene Fathers," First Series, volume 10, Edited by Philip Schaff, D.D., LL.D.

29 "Homilies on the Gospel of Saint Matthew," by John Crysostom, Homily LXXVII, Matt 24:33, 34, paragraph 6. From "Nicene and Post-Nicene Fathers," First Series, volume 10, Edited by Philip Schaff, D.D., LL.D.

CHAPTER 2

—◆◆◆—

Ancient Teaching That Bible Prophecy
Should be Interpreted Literally

An essential element of dispensationalism is to interpret explicit state-ments of Bible prophecy literally, as opposed to symbolically. This idea goes all the way back to the very beginnings of Christian teachings on the subject. This necessity was stressed by Justin Martyr,[30] one of the oldest Christian writers whose works have been preserved. He devoted an entire chapter to this subject in a work which is believed to have been written between A.D. 155 and 167.

> **"Since, then, we prove that all things which have already hap-pened had been predicted by the prophets before they came to pass, we must necessarily believe also that those things which are in like manner predicted, but are yet to come to pass, shall certainly happen.** For as the things which have already taken place came to pass when foretold, and even though unknown, so shall the things that remain, even though they be unknown and disbelieved, yet come to pass. For the prophets have proclaimed two advents of His: the one, that which is already past, when

---

30 All quotations of Justin Martyr in this book are from Volume 1 of "The Early Church Fathers: Ante-Nicene Fathers," edited by Alexander Roberts and James Donaldson, as found in its Ameri-can edition edited by A. Cleveland Coxe.

He came as a dishonoured and suffering Man; but the second, when, according to prophecy, He shall come from heaven with glory, accompanied by His angelic host, when also He shall raise the bodies of all men who have lived, and shall clothe those of the worthy with immortality, and shall send those of the wicked, endued with eternal sensibility, into everlasting fire with the wicked devils. And that these things also have been foretold as yet to be, we will prove. By Ezekiel the prophet it was said: "Joint shall be joined to joint, and bone to bone, and flesh shall grow again; and every knee shall bow to the Lord, and every tongue shall confess Him." And in what kind of sensation and punishment the wicked are to be, hear from what was said in like manner with reference to this; it is as follows: "Their worm shall not rest, and their fire shall not be quenched;" and then shall they repent, when it profits them not." ("The First Apology of Justin," by Justin Martyr, chapter 52.)

Irenaeus, who in his writings systematically interpreted the prophetic writings literally, insisted on the importance of this literal interpretation by saying:

"If, however, any shall endeavour to allegorize [prophecies] of this kind, they shall not be found consistent with themselves in all points, and shall be confuted by the teaching of the very expressions [in question]. For example: 'When the cities' of the Gentiles 'shall be desolate, so that they be not inhabited, and the houses so that there shall be no men in them and the land shall be left desolate.' 'For, behold,' says Isaiah, 'the day of the Lord cometh past remedy, full of fury and wrath, to lay waste the city of the earth, and to root sinners out of it.' And again he says, 'Let him be taken away, that he behold not the glory of God.' And when these things are done, he says, 'God will remove men far away, and those that are left shall multiply in the earth.' 'And they shall build houses, and shall inhabit them themselves: and plant vineyards, and eat of them themselves.'" ("Against Heresies," by Irenaeus, book V, chapter XXXV, paragraph 1.)

Irenaeus applied this principle in many passages, such as:

"From all these passages are revealed to us, not merely the particulars of the apostasy, and [the doings] of him who concentrates in himself every satanic error, but also, that there is one and the same God the Father, who was declared by the prophets, but made manifest by Christ. For if what Daniel prophesied concerning the end has been confirmed by the Lord, when He said, 'When ye shall see the abomination of desolation, which has been spoken of by Daniel the prophet' (and the angel Gabriel gave the interpretation of the visions to Daniel, and he is the archangel of the Creator (Demiurgi), who also proclaimed to Mary the visible coming and the incarnation of Christ), then one and the same God is most manifestly pointed out, who sent the prophets, and made promise of the Son, and called us into His knowledge. (Against Heresies, by Irenaeus, book V, chapter XXV, paragraph 5.)

"In a still clearer light has John, in the Apocalypse, indicated to the Lord's disciples what shall happen **in the last times**, and concerning **the ten kings who shall then arise, among whom the empire which now rules [the earth] shall be partitioned.** He teaches us what the ten horns shall be which were seen by Daniel, telling us that thus it had been said to him: 'And the ten horns which thou sawest are ten kings, who have received no kingdom as yet, but shall receive power as if kings one hour with the beast. These have one mind, and give their strength and power to the beast. These shall make war with the Lamb, and the Lamb shall overcome them, because He is the Lord of lords and the King of kings.' It is manifest, therefore, **that of these [potentates], he who is to come shall slay three, and subject the remainder to his power, and that he shall be himself the eighth among them. And they shall lay Babylon waste, and burn her with fire, and shall give their kingdom to the beast, and put the Church to flight.** After that they shall be destroyed by the coming of our Lord." (Against Heresies, by Irenaeus, book V, chapter XXVI, paragraph 1.)

"... the number of the name of the beast, [if reckoned] according to the Greek mode of calculation by the [value of] the letters contained in it, will amount to six hundred and sixty and six; that is, the number of tens shall be equal to that of the hundreds, and the number of hundreds equal to that of the units (for that number which [expresses] the digit six being adhered to throughout, indicates the recapitulations of that apostasy, taken in its full extent, which occurred at the beginning, during the intermediate periods, and which shall take place at the end), — I do not know how it is that some have erred following the ordinary mode of speech, and have vitiated the middle number in the name, deducting the amount of fifty from it, so that instead of six decads they will have it that there is but one. [I am inclined to think that this occurred through the fault of the copyists, as is wont to happen, since numbers also are expressed by letters; so that the Greek letter which expresses the number sixty was easily expanded into the letter Iota of the Greeks.] Others then received this reading without examination; some in their simplicity, and upon their own responsibility, making use of this number expressing one decad; while some, in their inexperience, have ventured to seek out a name which should contain the erroneous and spurious number. **Now, as regards those who have done this in simplicity, and without evil intent, we are at liberty to assume that pardon will be granted them by God. But as for those who, for the sake of vainglory, lay it down for certain that names containing the spurious number are to be accepted, and affirm that this name, hit upon by themselves, is that of him who is to come; such persons shall not come forth without loss, because they have led into error both themselves and those who confided in them. Now, in the first place, it is loss to wander from the truth, and to imagine that as being the case which is not; then again, as there shall be no light** punishment [inflicted] upon him who either adds or subtracts anything from the Scripture, under that such a person must necessarily fall." (Against Heresies, by Irenaeus, book V, chapter XXX, paragraph 1.)

"But when this Antichrist shall have devastated all things in this world, he will reign for three years and six months, and sit in the temple at Jerusalem; and then the Lord will come from heaven in the clouds, in the glory of the Father, sending this man and those who follow him into the lake of fire; but bringing in for the righteous the times of the kingdom, that is, the rest, the hallowed seventh day; and restoring to Abraham the promised inheritance, in which kingdom the Lord declared, that 'many coming from the east and from the west should sit down with Abraham, Isaac, and Jacob.' " (Against Heresies, by Irenaeus, book V, chapter XXX, paragraph 3.)

A practical application of this principle can also be seen in the following by Tertullian:

"But I will set before you more literal points. 'He shall have dominion,' says the Psalmist, 'from sea to sea, and from the river unto the ends of the earth.' To Christ alone was this given; whilst Solomon reigned over only the moderately-sized kingdom of Judah. 'Yea, all kings shall fall down before Him.' Whom, indeed, shall they all thus worship, except Christ? 'All nations shall serve Him.' To whom shall all thus do homage, but Christ? 'His name shall endure for ever.' Whose name has this eternity of fame, but Christ's? 'Longer than the sun shall His name remain,' for longer than the sun shall be the Word of God, even Christ. 'And in Him shall all nations be blessed.' In Solomon was no nation blessed; in Christ every nation. And what if the Psalm proves Him to be even God? 'They shall call Him blessed. (On what ground?) Because blessed Is the Lord God of Isreal, who only doeth wonderful things.' 'Blessed also is His glorious name, and with His glory shall all the earth be filled.' On the contrary, Solomon (as I make bold to affirm) lost even the glory which he had from God, seduced by his love of women even into idolatry. And thus, the statement which occurs in about the middle of this Psalm, 'His enemies shall lick the dust' (of course, as having been, (to use the apostle's phrase,) 'put under His feet'), will bear upon the very object which I had in view, when I both introduced the Psalm, and insisted on my opinion of its sense,—namely, that I might demonstrate both the glory of His kingdom and the subjection of His enemies in pursuance of the Creator's own plans, with the view of laying down this conclusion, that none but He can be believed to be the Christ of the Creator."[31]

Again Tertullian said:

"Now, to upset all conceits of this sort, let me dispel at once the preliminary idea on which they rest—their assertion that the prophets make all their announcements in figures of speech. Now, if this were the case, the figures themselves could not possibly have been distinguished, inasmuch as the verities would not have been declared, out of which the figurative language is stretched. And, indeed, if all are figures, where will be that of which they are the figures? How can you hold up a mirror for your face, if the face nowhere exists? But, in truth, all are not figures, but there are also literal statements; nor are all shadows, but there are bodies too: so that we have prophecies about the Lord Himself even, which are clearer than the day For it was not figuratively that the Virgin conceived in her womb; nor in a trope did she bear Emmanuel, that is, Jesus, God with us. **Even granting that He was figuratively to take the power of Damascus and the spoils of Samaria, still it was literally that He was to 'enter into judgment with the elders and princes of the people.'** For in the person of Pilate 'the

---

31 "The Five Books Against Marcion," by Tertullian, book 5, chapter 9, Translated by Dr. Holmes, from "The Early Church Fathers: Ante-Nicene Fathers," vol. 3, ed. by Alexander Roberts and James Donaldson, as found in its American edition ed. by A. Cleveland Coxe.

heathen raged,' and in the person of Isreal 'the people imagined vain things;' 'the kings of the earth' in Herod, and the rulers in Annas and Caiaphas, were 'gathered together against the Lord, and against His anointed.' He, again, was 'led as a sheep to the slaughter, and as a sheep before the shearer,' that is, Herod, 'is dumb, so He opened not His mouth.' 'He gave His back to scourges, and His cheeks to blows, not turning His face even from the shame of spitting.' 'He was numbered with the transgressors;' 'He was pierced in His hands and His feet;' 'they cast lots for his raiment' 'they gave Him gall, and made Him drink vinegar;' 'they shook their heads, and mocked Him;' 'He was appraised by the traitor in thirty pieces of silver.' **What figures of speech does Isaiah here give us? What tropes does David? What allegories does Jeremiah? Not even of His mighty works have they used parabolic language.** Or else, were not the eyes of the blind opened? did not the tongue of the dumb recover speech? did not the relaxed hands and palsied knees become strong, and the lame leap as an hart? **No doubt we are accustomed also to give a spiritual significance to these statements of prophecy, according to the analogy of the physical diseases which were healed by the Lord; but still they were all fulfilled literally: thus showing that the prophets foretold both senses, except that very many of their words can only be taken in a pure and simple signification, and free from all allegorical obscurity;** as when we hear of the downfall of nations and cities, of Tyre and Egypt, and Babylon and Edom, and the navy of Carthage; also when they foretell Isreal's own chastisements and pardons, its captivities, restorations, and at last its final dispersion. **Who would prefer affixing a metaphorical interpretation to all these events, instead of accepting their literal truth?** The realities are involved in the words, just as the words are read in the realities. **Thus, then, (we find that) the allegorical style is not used in all parts of the prophetic record, although it occasionally occurs in certain portions of it."**[32]

---

32 "On the Resurrection of the Flesh," by Tertullian, chapter 20, Translated by Dr. Holmes, from "The Early Church Fathers: Ante-Nicene Fathers," vol. 3, ed. by Alexander Roberts and James Donaldson, as found in its American edition ed. by A. Cleveland Coxe.

And he further said:

"Now, if even parables obscure not the light of the gospel, how unlikely it is that plain sentences and declarations, which have an unmistakeable meaning, should signify any other thing than their literal sense!" [33]

We next come to Hippolytus, who, writing, as it is thought, between the years 202 and 211 AD., [34] spoke assuredly of coming events, based on a literal interpretation of Bible prophecy, in places such as:

"For just as upon Sodom when their transgressions were fulfilled, immediately fire descended upon them and they were destroyed, **in this way it will be even now, when lawlessness multiplies in the world and the present iron beast is divided into ten horns and anarchy occurs and discord, while others from here and there rend the kingdom, then the end shall come upon them."**[35]

" 'But all these *things* are the beginning of birth pangs,' he says, 'But the end *is* not yet in them,' for first it is necessary for the Gospel of the Lord to be preached in the whole world for a witness to all nations and in this way the end shall come, when all at once the time is fulfilled." [36]

And, even as late as the turn of the fifth century, Augustin said:

"But in addition to the foregoing rule, which guards us against taking a metaphorical form of speech as if it were literal, we must also pay heed to that which tells us not to take a literal form of speech as if it were figurative. In the

---

33 Ibid, chapter 33.

34 The "Commentary on Daniel," by Hippolytus, is the very oldest Christian commentary on scripture that has survived to the present day.

35 "Commentary on Daniel," by Hippolytus, book 2, chapter 6, paragraph 4, from a draft copy of the forthcoming translation by T. C. Schmidt, which he personally provided to this writer. Used by permission.

36 Ibid, book 2, chapter 17.

first place, then, we must show the way to find out whether a phrase is literal or figurative." [37]

And finally, we come to Jerome, a contemporary of Augustin, who said concerning Daniel 7:8 that:

> **"We should therefore concur with the traditional interpretation of all the commentators of the Christian Church,** that at the end of the world, when the Roman Empire is to be destroyed, there shall be ten kings who will partition the Roman world amongst themselves. Then an insignificant eleventh king will arise, who will overcome three of the ten kings... Then after they have been slain, the seven other kings will bow their necks to the victor." [38]

We need to particularly notice the words here, that this is "**the traditional interpretation of all the commentators of the Christian Church.**" thus, we see that, at least according to the very famous Jerome, who produced the Vulgate translation of the Bible into Latin, this practice of interpreting the explicit statements of Bible prophecy literally, was not only still in use, but was the standard practice of "**all the commentators of the Christian Church,**" at least up to the fifth century, when Jerome wrote.

So we see that the earliest preserved writings of the church on Bible prophecy are full of, insistence upon, and examples of taking at face value, that is, of interpreting literally, explicit statements of events which the Bible says will come to pass. And that this was still the standard practice of Christian commentators at least up to the fifth century.

---

37 "On Christian Doctrine," by Augustin, translated by Richard Stothert, M.A., Bombay, book III, chapter 10, from "Nicene and Post-Nicene Fathers, first series, vol 4, ed. by Philip Schaff, D.D., LL.D.

38 Jerome's comments on Daniel 7:8, as found in "Jerome's Commentary on Daniel," by Jerome, pg. 77, translated by Gleason L. Archer, Jr., pub. by Baker Book House, Grand Rapids, 1958.

CHAPTER 3

———◆◆◆———

Ancient Teaching of an Unfulfilled
Prophetic Program for the Jews

Many insist that, in order to qualify as dispensationalism, a doctrine must teach a clear differentiation between Israel and the church. While this differentiation was never stressed in any ancient document currently known to this writer, its essence was taught in many of them. This can be seen in the fact that, although the end time blessing they taught for the church was at least similar to what is commonly taught today, the end time blessing they taught for the Jews was different. For they taught that the Jews will be brought back to their land and there restored to their God. As there was so very much ancient writing on this subject, it is here divided into two chapters. This chapter is about their being brought back to the land, and the next one about their spiritual restoration to their God.

The ancient Christian commentaries on Bible prophecy are filled with comments about the Jews being brought back to their land. It is critical to realize that these comments do not say "Israel," for many would interpret these to be references to "the church," under the theory that in Bible prophecy, "Israel" means "the church." But all but one of these many ancient comments did not say "Israel," but "the Jews," or occasionally, "the Hebrews" or "the circumcision." This leaves zero room for imagining that their writers actually meant "the church."

We will begin this discussion by examining the very oldest Christian commentary on Bible prophecy (of any significant length) that has survived to the present day. This, as we have noted previously, is the last 12 chapters of the very famous work by Irenaeus, titled, "Against Heresies." With the possible exceptions of the so-called "Epistle of Barnabas" and "The Shepherd of Hermas," this five volume work was circulated more widely in the early church than any other non-inspired document.

Irenaeus wrote on "The fraud, pride, and tyrannical kingdom of Antichrist, as described by Daniel and Paul," saying:

> "Moreover, he (the apostle) has also pointed out this which I have shown in many ways, that the temple in Jerusalem was made by the direction of the true God. For the apostle himself, speaking in his own person, distinctly called it the temple of God. Now I have shown in the third book, that no one is termed God by the apostles when speaking for themselves, except Him who truly is God, the Father of our Lord, by whose directions **the temple which is at Jerusalem** was constructed for those purposes which I have already mentioned; **in which [temple] the enemy shall sit, endeavouring to show himself as Christ**, as the Lord also declares: 'But when ye shall see the abomination of desolation, which has been spoken of by Daniel the prophet, standing in the holy place (let him that readeth understand), then let those who are in Judea flee into the mountains; and he who is upon the house-top, let him not come down to take anything out of his house: for there shall then be great hardship, such as has not been from the beginning of the world until now, nor ever shall be.' ("Against Heresies", by Irenaeus, book 5, chapter 25, "The fraud, pride, and tyrannical kingdom of Antichrist, as described by Daniel and Paul," paragraph 2.)

"The Lord also spoke as follows to those who did not believe in Him: 'I have come in my Father's name, and ye have not received Me: when another shall come in his own name, him ye will receive,' calling Antichrist 'the other,' because he is alienated from the Lord. This is also the unjust judge, whom the Lord mentioned as one 'who feared not God, neither regarded man,' to whom the widow fled in her forgetfulness of God, — **that is, the earthly Jerusalem, — to be avenged of her adversary. Which also he shall do in the time of his kingdom: he shall remove his kingdom into that [city], and shall sit in the temple of God,** leading astray those who worship him, as if he were Christ. To this purpose Daniel says again: 'And he shall desolate the holy place; and sin has been given for a sacrifice, and righteousness been cast away in the earth, and he has been active (fecit), and gone on prosperously.'" ("Against Heresies", by Irenaeus, book 5, chapter 25, "The fraud, pride, and tyrannical kingdom of Anti-christ, as described by Daniel and Paul," paragraph 4.)

Aside from how startlingly similar this is to many modern commentaries on this subject, we nee'd to notice the following details from these quotations:

1. In the first quotation (paragraph 2) he stressed that the temple in which the Antichrist would sit was "**the temple in Jerusalem,**" that this would be "**the temple of God,**" and that "**those who are in Judea**" should flee when that happens.

2. In the second quotation (from just two paragraphs later) he said that those who heard Jesus, but did not accept him, (that is, the Jews) would accept the Antichrist, and interprets "**the unjust judge**" to represent "**the earthly Jerusalem.**" He further says that the Antichrist would "**remove his kingdom into that [city]**" and sit in "**the temple of God,**" which he had, just two paragraphs earlier, defined as "**the temple in Jerusalem.**"

We next come to a statement by Tertullian which is thought to have been written in the year A.D. 208:

> **"Besides, your Christ promises to the Jews their primitive condition, with the recovery of their country;** and after this life's course is over, repose in Hades in Abraham's bosom. Oh, most excellent God, when He restores in amnesty what He took away in wrath! Oh, what a God is yours, who both wounds and heals, creates evil and makes peace! Oh, what a God, that is merciful even down to Hades! in Abraham's bosom. Oh, most excellent God, when He restores in amnesty what He took away in wrath! Oh, what a God is yours, who both wounds and heals, creates evil and makes peace! Oh, what a God, that is merciful even down to Hades! I shall have something to say about Abraham's bosom in the proper place. As for the restoration of Judea, however, which even the Jews themselves, induced by the names of places and countries, hope for just as it is described, it would be tedious to state at length how the figurative interpretation is spiritually applicable to Christ and His church, and to the character and fruits thereof; besides, the subject has been regularly treated in another work, which we entitle De Spe Fidelium. At present, too, it would be superfluous for this reason, that our inquiry relates to what is promised in heaven, not on earth. But we do confess that a kingdom is promised to us upon the earth, although before heaven, only in another state of existence; inasmuch as it will be after the resurrection for a thousand years in the divinely-built city of Jerusalem, "let down from heaven," which the apostle also calls "our mother from above; " and, while declaring that our πολίτευμα, or citizenship, is in heaven, he predicates of it that it is really a city in heaven. This both Ezekiel had knowledge of and the Apostle John beheld." [39]

---

39 "The Five Books Against Marcion," by Tertullian, book 3, chapter 25, "Christ's Millennial and Heavenly Glory in Company with His Saints," from "The Early Church Fathers: Ante-Nicene Fathers," vol. 3, ed. by Alexander Roberts and James Donaldson, as found in its American edition ed. by A. Cleveland Coxe.

Here, Tertullian was denouncing another for interpreting literally the Bible prophecies concerning the restoration of the Jews to "**their primitive condition**," and basically teaching "Replacement Theology." But his very argument shows that this was being taught at that time.

We next come to Hippolytus, who is thought to have written the following between the years A.D. 202 and 211. He said:

> "And so these *things* the prophet described in this way concerning the Antichrist, as he will be shameless and warlike and a tyrant daring to exalt himself over every god, who boasts in his own power and pillages the fortresses of cities, and bearing lofty *things* in gold and silver and precious stone, he shall speak immoderate words against God, wishing that he himself alone be worshiped as God.

> "Concerning him all Scripture is not silent and the prophets announced beforehand his coming for the destruction of many, and the Lord has testified to these *things*, and the apostles taught these *things* concerning him, and John in the Apocalypse mystically revealed his name through a number.

> "The Lord displayed this abomination of desolation and the apostle taught that this son of the devil arrives according to the working of Satan.

> "This one, having struck the city of Tyre, will also desolate the land of Egypt, having waged war he will extend and destroy all the land of Libya, *and* he shall ruin the kingdom of the Ethiopians with his might in the slaughter of the sword.

> "**He, being lifted up over every king and every god, shall build the city of Jerusalem and he shall raise the converted Temple, he shall restore both all the land and its borders to the Jews, and having summoned their people from the slavery of the nations, he shall exhibit himself to them as king, and at this the faithless shall worship him as God and shall bend the knee to him, considering him to be the Christ, not**

apprehending what was spoken by the prophet, how he is a deceiver and not truth." [40]

Here, we need to notice the words that "he shall restore both all the land and its borders to the Jews, and having summoned their people from the slavery of the nations, he shall exhibit himself to them as king."

Again, in what appears to be a different document, Hippolytus said:

"Thus, then, does the prophet set forth these things concerning the Antichrist, who shall be shameless, a war-maker, and despot, **who, exalting himself above all kings and above every god, shall build the city of Jerusalem, and restore the sanctuary."** [41]

So here again, Hipplytus said that the Antichrist "shall build the city of Jerusalem, and restore the sanctuary."

Hippolytus also wrote the following series:

"Then he says: 'A fourth beast, dreadful and terrible; it had iron teeth and claws of brass.' And who are these but the Romans? which (kingdom) is meant by the iron—the kingdom which is now established; for the legs of that (image) were of iron. And after this, what remains, beloved, but the toes of the feet of the image, in which part is iron and part clay, mixed together? And mystically by the toes of the feet he meant the kings who are to arise from among them; as Daniel also says (in the words), 'I considered the beast, and lo there were ten horns behind it, among which shall rise another (horn), an offshoot, and shall pluck up by the roots the three (that were) before it.' **And under this was signified none other than Antichrist, who is also himself to raise the kingdom of the Jews.** He says that three horns are plucked up by the root by him, viz., the three kings of Egypt,

---

40 "Commentary on Daniel," by Hippolytus, Book 4, 49.1-49.5, from a draft copy of the forthcoming translation by T. C. Schmidt, which he personally provided to this writer. Used by permission.

41 "On Daniel," by Hippolytus, part 2, paragraph 39, from "The Early Church Fathers: Ante-Nicene Fathers," vol. 5, ed. by Alexander Roberts and James Donaldson, as found in its American edition ed. by A. Cleveland Coxe.

and Libya, and Ethiopia, whom he cuts off in the array of battle. And he, after gaining terrible power over all, being nevertheless a tyrant, shall stir up tribulation and persecution against men, exalting himself against them. For Daniel says: 'I considered the horn, and behold that horn made war with the saints, and prevailed against them, till the beast was slain and perished, and its body was given to the burning of fire.'" [42]

Here we need to notice the words, "Antichrist, who is also himself to raise the kingdom of the Jews."

"As his tribe, then, and his manifestation, and his destruction, have been set forth in these words, and as his name has also been indicated mystically, let us look also at his action. **For he will call together all the people to himself, out of every country of the dispersion, making them his own, as though they were his own children, and promising to restore their country, and establish again their kingdom and nation, in order that he may be worshipped by them as God,** as the prophet says: 'He will collect his whole kingdom, from the rising of the sun even to its setting: they whom he summons and they whom he does not summon shall march with him.' And Jeremiah speaks of him thus in a parable: 'The partridge cried, (and) gathered what he did not hatch, making himself riches without judgment: in the midst of his days they shall leave him, and at his end he shall be a fool.'" [43]

Here we see that Hippolytus taught that the Antichrist would gather **"all the people... out of every country of the dispersion."** This term **"the dispersion,"** or "the diaspora," as it is commonly called today, speaks specifically of the Jews who had been driven out of their land. But he went on to say that the Antichrist would promise **"to restore their country, and**

---

42 "Treatise on Christ and Antichrist," by Hippolytus, paragraph 25, from "The Early Church Fathers: Ante-Nicene Fathers," vol. 5, ed. by Alexander Roberts and James Donaldson, as found in its American edition ed. by A. Cleveland Coxe.

43 Ibid, paragraph 54.

establish again their kingdom and nation." Thus, he was obviously and explicitly speaking of an end time regathering of the Jews into their own ancient homeland.

> "By the unrighteous judge, who fears not God, neither regards man, he means without doubt Antichrist, as he is a son of the devil and a vessel of Satan. For when he has the power, he will begin to exalt himself against God, neither in truth fearing God, nor regarding the Son of God, who is the Judge of all. **And in saying that there was a widow in the city, he refers to Jerusalem itself,** which is a widow indeed, forsaken of her perfect, heavenly spouse, God. She calls Him her adversary, and not her Saviour; for she does not understand that which was said by the prophet Jeremiah: 'Because they obeyed not the truth, a spirit of error shall speak then to this people and to Jerusalem.'" [44]

Here, Hippolytus interpreted the unjust judge to be the Antichrist, and the widow whom he would not defend to be Jerusalem. And again we read:

> "Next he tells us of the 'fourth beast, dreadful and terrible; its teeth were of iron, and its claws of brass.' And what is meant by these but the kingdom of the Romans, which also is meant by the iron, by which it will crush all the seats of empire that were before it, and will lord it over the whole earth? After this, then, what is left for us to interpret of all that the prophet saw, but the 'toes of the image, in which part was of iron and part of clay, mingled together in one?' For by the ten toes of the image he meant figuratively the ten kings who sprang out of it, as Daniel also interpreted the matter. For he says, 'I considered the beast, namely the fourth; and behold ten horns after it, among which another horn arose like an offshoot; and it will pluck up by the root three of those before it.' **And by this offshoot horn none other is signified than the Antichrist that is to restore the kingdom of the Jews.** And the three horns which are to be rooted out by it signify three kings, namely

---

44   Ibid, paragraph 57.

those of Egypt, Libya, and Ethiopia, whom he will destroy in the array of war; and when he has vanquished them all, being a savage tyrant, he will raise tribulation and persecution against the saints, exalting himself against them." [45]

Here, in a document attributed to Hippolytus, we find the statement that the Antichrist "**is to restore the kingdom of the Jews.**"

"But seeing now that we must make proof of what is alleged at greater length, we shall not shrink from the task. For it is certain that he is destined to spring from the tribe of Dan, and to range himself in opposition like a princely tyrant, a terrible judge and accuser, as the prophet testifies when he says, 'Dan shall judge his people, as one tribe in Israel.' But some one may say that this was meant of Samson, who sprang from the tribe of Dan, and judged his people for twenty years. That, however, was only partially made good in the case of Samson; but this shall be fulfilled completely in the case of Antichrist. For Jeremiah, too, speaks in this manner: 'From Dan we shall hear the sound of the sharpness of his horses; at the sound of the neighing of his horses the whole land trembled.' And again, Moses says: 'Dan is a lion's whelp, and he shall leap from Bashan.' And that no one may fall into the mistake of thinking that this is spoken of the Saviour, let him attend to this. 'Dan,' says he, 'is a lion's whelp;' and by thus naming the tribe of Dan as the one whence the accuser is destined to spring, he made the matter in hand quite clear. For as Christ is born of the tribe of Judah, so Antichrist shall be born of the tribe of Dan. And as our Lord and Saviour Jesus Christ, the Son of God, was spoken of in prophecy as a lion on account or His royalty and glory, in the same manner also has the Scripture prophetically described the accuser as a lion, on account of his tyranny and violence." [46]

---

45   "A discourse by the most blessed Hippolytus, bishop and martyr, on the end of the world, and on Antichrist, and on the second coming of our lord Jesus Christ." alleged to be by Hippolytus, paragraph 16, from "Appendix to the Works of Hippolytus, Containing Dubious and Spurious Pieces" in "The Early Church Fathers: Ante-Nicene Fathers," vol. 5, ed. by Alexander Roberts and James Donaldson, as found in its American edition ed. by A. Cleveland Coxe.

46   Ibid, paragraph 19.

Here we see Hippolytus, or (again) some other ancient writer alleged to be Hippolytus, teaching that the Antichrist would be "**from the tribe of Dan,**" that is, an Israelite, rather than a Roman, as many make him out to be. (For our purposes, it does not matter whether or not these comments were actually written by Hippolytus, for our only point is to see that this was taught in that general time period.)

"For in every respect that deceiver seeks to make himself appear like the Son of God. Christ is a lion, and Antichrist is a lion. Christ is King of things celestial and things terrestrial, and Antichrist will be king upon earth. The Saviour was manifested as a lamb; and he, too, will appear as a lamb, while he is a wolf within.

The Saviour was circumcised, and he in like manner will appear in circumcision. The Saviour sent the apostles unto all the nations, and he in like manner will send false apostles. Christ gathered together the dispersed sheep, and he in like manner will gather together the dispersed people of the Hebrews. Christ gave to those who believed on Him the honourable and life-giving cross, and he in like manner will give his own sign. Christ appeared in the form of man, and he in like manner will come forth in the form of man. Christ arose from among the Hebrews, and he will spring from among the Jews. Christ displayed His flesh like a temple, and raised it up on the third day; and he too will raise up again the temple of stone in Jerusalem. And these deceits fabricated by him will become quite intelligible to those who listen to us attentively, from what shall be set forth next in order." [47]

Here we see this unknown writer alleged to have been Hippolytus explicitly saying that the Antichrist "**will gather together the dispersed people of the Hebrews,**" that he will come "**in circumcision,**" and that "**he will spring from among the Jews.**"

And each of the following is also alleged to be by Hippolytus:

47 Ibid, paragraph 20.

"Above all, moreover, he will love the nation of the Jews. And with all these he will work signs and terrible wonders, false wonders and not true, in order to deceive his impious equals. For if it were possible, he would seduce even the elect from the love of Christ. But in his first steps he will be gentle, loveable, quiet, pious, pacific, hating injustice, detesting gifts, not allowing idolatry; loving, says he, the Scriptures, reverencing priests, honouring his elders, repudiating fornication, detesting adultery, giving no heed to slanders, not admitting oaths, kind to strangers, kind to the poor, compassionate. And then he will work wonders, cleansing lepers, raising paralytics, expelling demons, proclaiming things remote just as things present, raising the dead, helping widows, defending orphans, loving all, reconciling in love men who contend, and saying to such, 'Let not the sun go down upon your wrath; ' and he will not acquire gold, nor love silver, nor seek riches." [48]

"And all this he will do corruptly and deceitfully, and with the purpose of deluding all to make him king. For when the peoples and tribes see so great virtues and so great powers in him, they will all with one mind meet together to make him king. **And above all others shall the nation of the Hebrews be dear to the tyrant himself, while they say one to another, Is there found indeed in our generation such a man, so good and just? That shall be the way with the race of the Jews pre-eminently, as I said before, who, thinking, as they do, that they shall behold the king himself in such power, will approach him to say, We all confide in thee, and acknowledge thee to be just upon the whole earth; we all hope to be saved by thee; and by thy mouth we have received just and incorruptible judgment."** [49]

"And at first, indeed, that deceitful and lawless one, with crafty deceitfulness, will refuse such glory; but the men persisting, and

---

48 Ibid, paragraph 23.
49 Ibid, paragraph 24.

holding by him, will declare him king. And thereafter he will be lifted up in heart, and he who was formerly gentle will become violent, and he who pursued love will become pitiless, and the humble in heart will become haughty and inhuman, and the hater of unrighteousness will persecute the righteous. Then, when he is elevated to his kingdom, he will marshal war; and in his wrath he will smite three mighty kings,—those, namely, of Egypt, Libya, and Ethiopia. **And after that he will build the temple in Jerusalem, and will restore it again speedily, and give it over to the Jews.** And then he will be lifted up in heart against every man; yea, he will speak blasphemy also against God, thinking in his deceit that he shall be king upon the earth hereafter for ever; not knowing, miserable wretch, that his kingdom is to be quickly brought to nought, and that he will quickly have to meet the fire which is prepared for him, along with all who trust him and serve him." [50]

We have seen each of the following concepts repeatedly taught in this long series attributed to Hippolytus. First, that the Antichrist will build the temple and the city of Jerusalem. Second, that he will call the Jews back to their land and restore the kingdom to them. Third, that he will spring from among the Jews, and in particular, from the tribe of Dan.

We now come to Cyril of Jerusalem, who is believed to have written the following sometime around the year A.D. 350:

"11. But as, when formerly He was to take man's nature, and God was expected to be born of a Virgin, the devil created prejudice against this, by craftily preparing among idol-worshippers fables of false gods, begetting and begotten of women, that, the falsehood having come first, the truth, as he supposed, might be disbelieved; so now, since the true Christ is to come a second time, **the adversary, taking occasion by the expectation of the simple, and especially of them of the circumcision, brings in a certain man who is a magician, and most expert in sorceries**

---

50 Ibid, paragraph 25.

and enchantments of beguiling craftiness; who shall seize for himself the power of the Roman empire, and shall falsely style himself Christ; by this name of Christ deceiving the Jews, who are looking for the Anointed, and seducing those of the Gentiles by his magical illusions.

"12. But this aforesaid Antichrist is to come when the times of the Roman empire shall have been fulfilled, and the end of the world is now drawing near. There shall rise up together ten kings of the Romans, reigning in different parts perhaps, but all about the same time; and after these an eleventh, the Antichrist, who by his magical craft shall seize upon the Roman power; and of the kings who reigned before him, three he shall humble, and the remaining seven he shall keep in subjection to himself. At first indeed he will put on a show of mildness (as though he were a learned and discreet person), and of soberness and benevolence: **and by the lying signs and wonders of his magical deceit having beguiled the Jews, as though he were the expected Christ, he shall afterwards be characterized by all kinds of crimes of inhumanity and lawlessness, so as to outdo all unrighteous and ungodly men who have gone before him;** displaying against all men, but especially against us Christians, a spirit murderous and most cruel, merciless and crafty. And after perpetrating such things for three years and six months only, he shall be destroyed by the glorious second advent from heaven of the only-begotten Son of God, our Lord and Saviour Jesus, the true Christ, who shall slay Antichrist with the breath of His mouth , and shall deliver him over to the fire of hell.

"13. Now these things we teach, not of our own invention, but having learned them out of the divine Scriptures used in the Church, and chiefly from the prophecy of Daniel just now read; as Gabriel also the Archangel interpreted it, speaking thus: The fourth beast shall be a fourth kingdom upon earth, which shall surpass all kingdoms. And that this kingdom is that of the Romans, has been the tradition of the Church's interpreters. For as the first kingdom which became renowned was that of the

Assyrians, and the second, that of the Medes and Persians together, and after these, that of the Macedonians was the third,
so the fourth kingdom now is that of the Romans. Then Gabriel
goes on to interpret, saying, His ten horns are ten kings that
shall arise; and another king shall rise up after them, who shall
surpass in wickedness all who were before him; (he says, not
only the ten, but also all who have been before him;) and he
shall subdue three kings; manifestly out of the ten former kings:
but it is plain that by subduing three of these ten, he will become the eighth king; and he shall speak words against the Most
High. A blasphemer the man is and lawless, not having received
the kingdom from his fathers, but having usurped the power by
means of sorcery.

"14. And who is this, and from what sort of working? Interpret
to us, O Paul. Whose coming, he says, is after the working of
Satan, with all power and signs and lying wonders; implying,
that Satan has used him as an instrument, working in his own
person through him; for knowing that his judgment shall now
no longer have respite, he wages war no more by his ministers, as
is his wont, but henceforth by himself more openly. And with all
signs and lying wonders; for the father of falsehood will make a
show of the works of falsehood, that the multitudes may think
that they see a dead man raised, who is not raised, and lame
men walking, and blind men seeing, when the cure has not been
wrought.

"15. And again he says, Who opposeth and exalteth himself
against all that is called God, or that is worshipped; (against
every God; Antichrist forsooth will abhor the idols,) **so that he
seateth himself in the temple of God. What temple then? He
means, the Temple of the Jews which has been destroyed. For
God forbid that it should be the one in which we are! Why say
we this? That we may not be supposed to favour ourselves. For
if he comes to the Jews as Christ, and desires to be worshipped
by the Jews, he will make great account of the Temple, that he
may more completely beguile them; making it supposed that**

he is the man of the race of David, who shall build up the Temple which was erected by Solomon. And Antichrist will come at the time when there shall not be left one stone upon another in the Temple of the Jews, according to the doom pronounced by our Saviour; for when, either decay of time, or demolition ensuing on pretence of new buildings, or from any other causes, shall have overthrown all the stones, I mean not merely of the outer circuit, but of the inner shrine also, where the Cherubim were, then shall he come with all signs and lying wonders, exalting himself against all idols; at first indeed making a pretence of benevolence, but afterwards displaying his relentless temper, and that chiefly against the Saints of God. For he says, I beheld, and the same horn made war with the saints; and again elsewhere, there shall be a time of trouble, such as never was since there was a nation upon earth, even to that same time. Dreadful is that beast, a mighty dragon, unconquerable by man, ready to devour; concerning whom though we have more things to speak out of the divine Scriptures, yet we will content ourselves at present with thus much, in order to keep within compass." [51]

In this rather long quotation, we first see, in paragraph 11, that Cyril taught the Antichrist as a Roman ruler who would deceive the Jews. Then, in paragraph 12, he said that this Antichrist would beguile the Jews. And, as a sort of a side note, he said in paragraph 13 that **"these things we teach, not of our own invention, but having learned them out of the divine Scriptures used in the Church,"** adding that the interpretation he put upon them **"has been the tradition of the Church's interpreters."** And finally, in paragraph 15, He very explicitly said that the temple in which Antichrist would sit would be **"the Temple of the Jews which has been destroyed,"** adding, **"if he comes to the Jews as Christ, and desires to be worshipped by the Jews, he will make great account of the Temple, that he may more completely beguile them;**

---

51   "The Catechetical Lectures of our Holy Father, Cyril, Archbishop of Jerusalem," by Cyril of Jerusalem, Lecture XV - "On the Clause, And Shall Come in Glory to Judge the Quick and the Dead; Of Whose Kingdom There Shall Be No End," paragraphs 11-15, from "Nicene and Post-Nicene Fathers, second series, vol. 7, ed. Philip Schaff, D.D., LL.D. and Henry Wace, D.D.

making it supposed that he is the man of the race of David, who shall build up the Temple which was erected by Solomon." And finally, he noted that "Antichrist will come at the time when there shall not be left one stone upon another in the Temple of the Jews."

We need to particularly notice Cyril's words that what he was teaching "has been the tradition of the Church's interpreters."

We see this restoration of Israel "to its kingdom" again in the writing of Hilary of Poitiers, who is thought to have penned the following sometime between the years A.D. 356 and 360:

> "Remember, God the Father set the day within His authority, that it might not come to the knowledge of man, and the Son, when asked before, replied that He did not know, but now, no longer denying His knowledge, replies that it is theirs not to know, for the Father has set the times not in His own knowledge, but in His own authority. **The day and the moment are included in the word 'times': can it be, then, that He, Who was to restore Israel to its kingdom, did not Himself know the day and the moment of that restoration?** He instructs us to see an evidence of His birth in this exclusive prerogative of the Father, yet He does not deny that He knows: and while He proclaims that the possession of this knowledge is withheld from ourselves, He asserts that it belongs to the mystery of the Father's authority." [52]

In this series of quotations we have seen that many ancient writers explicitly taught a physical return of "the Jews," to their ancient homeland, but sometimes calling them "the Hebrews," "the circumcision," or (only in the final quotation) "Israel."

---

52 "On the Trinity," by Hilary of Poitiers, book IX, paragraph 75, from "Nicene and Post-Nicene Fathers, second series, vol. 7, ed. Philip Schaff, D.D., LL.D. and Henry Wace, D.D.

CHAPTER 4

—◆◆◆—

Ancient Teaching of an End Time
Spiritual Restoration or Revival of Israel

But the ancient Christians not only taught that the Jews would be brought back to their land. Some of them also very explicitly spoke of an end time spiritual restoration or revival of Israel. The oldest of these known to this writer was Justin Martyr, who is believed to have written the following sometime between the years A.D. 155 and 167:

> **"And what the people of the Jews shall say and do, when they see Him coming in glory, has been thus predicted by Zechariah the prophet:** "I will command the four winds to gather the scattered children; I will command the north wind to bring them, and the south wind, that it keep not back. **And then in Jerusalem there shall be great lamentation, not the lamentation of mouths or of lips, but the lamentation of the heart; and they shall rend not their garments, but their hearts. Tribe by tribe they shall mourn, and then they shall look on Him whom they have pierced; and they shall say, Why, O Lord, hast Thou made us to err from Thy way? The glory which our fathers blessed, has for us been turned into shame."** ("The First Apology of Justin," by Justin Martyr, chapter 52, "Certain Fulfillment of Prophecy.")

So in this passage, Justin Martyr clearly interpreted the general mourning described in Zechariah 12:10-14 to an end time repentance of **"the people of the Jews."**

But this was not only taught in one of the very oldest surviving Christian comments on Bible prophecy. By the fifth century it had become a standard understanding of Christian teachers. For Augustin wrote:

> "After admonishing them to give heed to the law of Moses, as he foresaw that for a long time to come they would not understand it spiritually and rightly, he went on to say, 'And, behold, I will send to you Elias the Tishbite before the great and signal day of the Lord come: and he shall turn the heart of the father to the son, and the heart of a man to his next of kin, lest I come and utterly smite the earth.' **It is a familiar theme in the conversation and heart of the faithful, that in the last days before the judgment the Jews shall believe in the true Christ, that is, our Christ, by means of this great and admirable prophet Elias who shall expound the law to them. For not without reason do we hope that before the coming of our Judge and Saviour Elias shall come, because we have good reason to believe that he is now alive; for, as Scripture most distinctly informs us, he was taken up from this life in a chariot of fire. When, therefore, he is come, he shall give a spiritual explanation of the law which the Jews at present understand carnally, and shall thus 'turn the heart of the father to the son,' that is, the heart of fathers to their children; for the Septuagint translators have frequently put the singular for the plural number. And the meaning is, that the sons, that is, the Jews, shall understand the law as the fathers, that is, the prophets, and among them Moses himself, understood it.** For the heart of the fathers shall be turned to their children when the children understand the law as their fathers did; and the heart of the children shall be turned to their fathers when they have the same sentiments as the fathers. The Septuagint used the expression, 'and the heart of a man to his next of kin,' because fathers and children are eminently neighbors to one another. Another and a preferable

sense can be found in the words of the Septuagint translators, who have translated Scripture with an eye to prophecy, the sense, viz., that Elias shall turn the heart of God the Father to the Son, not certainly as if he should bring about this love of the Father for the Son, but meaning that he should make it known, and that **the Jews also, who had previously hated, should then love the Son who is our Christ. For so far as regards the Jews, God has His heart turned away from our Christ, this being their conception about God and Christ. But in their case the heart of God shall be turned to the Son when they themselves shall turn in heart, and learn the love of the Father towards the Son.** The words following, 'and the heart of a man to his next of kin,'—that is, Elias shall also turn the heart of a man to his next of kin,—how can we understand this better than as the heart of a man to the man Christ? For though in the form of God He is our God, yet, taking the form of a servant, He condescended to become also our next of kin. It is this, then, which Elias will do, 'lest,' he says, 'I come and smite the earth utterly.' For they who mind earthly things are the earth. Such are the carnal Jews until this day; and hence these murmurs of theirs against God, 'The wicked are pleasing to Him,' and 'It is a vain thing to serve God.'" [53]

Here we need to particularly notice Augustin's words, that "**It is a familiar theme in the conversation and heart of the faithful, that in the last days before the judgment the Jews shall believe in the true Christ, that is, our Christ.**" This is particularly important because it shows, not only that Augustin believed this, but that he said that this was being commonly taught by the Christian writers of Augustin's day.

In the same work Augustin also said:

"In like manner the Lord, speaking by the same prophet, says, 'And it shall come to pass in that day, that I will seek to destroy all the nations that come against Jerusalem. And I will pour upon the house of David, and upon the inhabitants of Jerusalem, the spirit of grace and mercy; and they shall look upon me because they have insulted me, and they shall mourn for Him as for one very dear, and shall be in bitterness as for an only-begotten.' To whom but to God does it belong to destroy all the nations that are hostile to the holy city Jerusalem, which 'come against it,' that is, are opposed to it, or, as some translate, 'come upon it,' as if putting it down under them; or to pour out upon the house of David and the inhabitants of Jerusalem the spirit of grace and mercy? This belongs doubtless to God, and it is to God the prophet ascribes the words; and yet Christ shows that He is the God who does these so great and divine things, when He goes on to say, 'And they shall look upon me because they have insulted me, and they shall mourn for Him as if for one very dear (or beloved), and shall be in bitterness for Him as for an only-begotten.' **For in that day the Jews—those of them, at least, who shall receive the spirit of grace and mercy—when they see Him coming in His majesty, and recognize that it is He whom they, in the person of their parents, insulted when He came before in His humiliation, shall repent of insulting Him in His passion:** and their parents themselves, who were the perpetrators of this huge impiety, shall see Him when they rise; but this will be only for their punishment, and not for their correction. It is not of them we are to understand the words, 'And I will pour upon the house of David, and upon the inhabitants of Jerusalem, the spirit of grace and mercy, and they shall look upon me because they have insulted me;' but we are to understand the words of their descendants, who shall at that time believe through Elias." [54]

Here, like Justin Martyr, Augustin applied Zechariah 12:10-14 to the Jews, saying, "For in that day the Jews—those of them, at least, who shall receive the spirit of grace and mercy—when they see Him coming in His majesty, and recognize that it is He whom they, in the person of their parents,

---

54   Ibid, chapter 30.

insulted when He came before in His humiliation, shall repent of insulting Him in His passion:" and then he noted that this prophecy did not speak of those who rejected Christ when He came, but of their descendants.

Further down in the same chapter, Augustin added:

> "That the last judgment, then, shall be administered by Jesus Christ in the manner predicted in the sacred writings is denied or doubted by no one, unless by those who, through some incredible animosity or blindness, decline to believe these writings, though already their truth is demonstrated to all the world. **And at or in connection with that judgment the following events shall come to pass, as we have learned: Elias the Tishbite shall come; the Jews shall believe; Antichrist shall persecute; Christ shall judge; the dead shall rise; the good and the wicked shall be separated; the world shall be burned and renewed. All these things, we believe, shall come to pass; but how, or in what order, human understanding cannot perfectly teach us, but only the experience of the events themselves. My opinion, however, is, that they will happen in the order in which I have related them."** [55]

Here again, Augustin clearly states "**Elias the Tishbite shall come;**" and "**the Jews shall believe,**" as the first two of the end time events he foresaw.

So we see that this concept was indeed taught in some of the earliest Christian writings on the subject, and had become established doctrine of the Church by the fifth century.

---

55   Ibid, chaprter 30.

CHAPTER 5

---◆◆◆---

Ancient Teaching that Daniel's
Seventieth Week Has Not Been Fulfilled

The concept of a future fulfillment of Daniel's seventieth week is an essential part of Dispensational doctrine, and is totally incompatible with all other forms of prophetic interpretation, such as Covenant Theology, Historicism, Preterism, and Idealism. So it may come as a total surprise to many, as it was to this writer, that this was taught, and very clearly taught, in some of the oldest Christian commentaries that have survived to the present day.

The very oldest Christian commentary on Bible prophecy (of any significant length) that has survived to the present day is the last twelve chapters of the very famous five volume work by Irenaeus titled "Against Heresies," which is thought to have been published between the years A.D. 186 and 188:

Irenaeus wrote:

> "And the angel Gabriel, when explaining his vision, states with regard to this person: 'And towards the end of their kingdom a king of a most fierce countenance shall arise, one understanding [dark] questions, and exceedingly powerful, full of wonders; and he shall corrupt, direct, influence (faciet), and put strong men down, the holy people likewise; and his yoke shall be directed as a wreath [round their neck]; deceit shall be in his hand, and he shall be lifted up in his heart: he shall also ruin many by deceit, and lead many to perdition, bruising them in his hand like eggs.'

And then he points out the time that his tyranny shall last, during which the saints shall be put to flight, they who offer a pure sacrifice unto God: 'And in the midst of the week,' he says, 'the sacrifice and the libation shall be taken away, and the abomination of desolation [shall be brought] into the temple: even unto the consummation of the time shall the desolation be complete.' Now three years and six months constitute the half-week. ("Against Heresies", by Irenaeus, book 5, chapter 25, "The fraud, pride, and tyrannical kingdom of Antichrist, as described by Daniel and Paul," paragraph 4.)

Here we see Irenaeus, in describing the events he foresaw as coming in the future, explicitly quoting from Daniel's prophecy of the seventieth week, saying, **"And in the midst of the week,' he says, 'the sacrifice and the libation shall be taken away, and the abomination of desolation [shall be brought] into the temple: even unto the consummation of the time shall the desolation be complete."** This is a quotation of Daniel 9:27, the last verse of Daniel's discussion of what would take place in the seventy weeks of his prophecy. We should note here that the modern practice of using only the exact words of the original in a quotation, simply did not exist at this time. Even in the Bible, there are many quotations in which the original wording has been slightly altered.

Five chapters later, Irenaeus again mentioned this half week:

"But when this Antichrist shall have devastated all things in this world, he will reign for three years and six months, and sit in the temple at Jerusalem; and then the Lord will come from heaven in the clouds, in the glory of the Father, sending this man and those who follow him into the lake of fire; but bringing in for the righteous the times of the kingdom, that is, the rest, the hallowed seventh day; and restoring to Abraham the promised inheritance, in which kingdom the Lord declared, that 'many coming from the east and from the west should sit down with Abraham, Isaac, and Jacob.'" ("Against Heresies", by Irenaeus, book 5, chapter 30, paragraph 4.)

Hippolytus wrote even more clearly on this in the very oldest Christian commentary on scripture which has survived to the present day. This was a commentary on Daniel which is thought to have been written between A.D. 202 and 211:

Hippolytus wrote:

> **"For after sixty-two weeks was fulfilled and after Christ has come and the Gospel has been preached in every place, times having been spun out, the end remains one week away**, in which Elijah and Enoch shall be present and in its half the abomination of desolation, the Antichrist, shall appear who threatens desolation of the world.
>
> After he comes, sacrifice and drink offering, which now in every way is offered by the nations to God, shall be taken away." [56]

And again, fifteen chapters later, Hippolytus also wrote:

> **"Just as also he spoke to Daniel, "And he shall establish a covenant with many for one week and it will be that in the half of the week he shall take away my sacrifice and drink offering," so that the one week may be shown as divided into two, after the two witnesses will have preached for three and a half years, the Antichrist will wage war against the saints the remainder of the week and will desolate all the world so that what was spoken may be fulfilled,** "And they will give the abomination of desolation one thousand two hundred ninety days. Blessed is he who endures to Christ and reaches the one thousand three hundred thirty-five days!" [57]

So Hippolytus not only taught that Daniel's seventieth week remained to be fulfilled in the future. He said **"the one week may be shown as divided in two."** And then said, **"after the two witnesses will have preached for**

---

56 "Commentary on Daniel", by Hippolytus, book 4, 35.3, from a draft copy of the forthcoming translation by T. C. Schmidt, which he personally provided to this writer. Used by permission.

57 Ibid, book 4, 50.2.

three and a half years, the Antichrist will wage war against the saints the remainder of the week."

Hippolytus also explained how this fits with other statements of time in the prophetic scriptures, writing:

> "But he, wishing to persuade these according to every way, raised his right hand and his left hand to heaven and swore by him who lives forever.
>
> "What and to whom did he swear? The Son *swore* to Father, saying that the Father lives forever *and that* they truly shall know all these *things* in a time and times and half of a time, when the dispersal *of the Jews* has been consummated.
>
> "And so he stretched out his hands, *and* through this he displayed the passion.
>
> **"But when he says, 'In a time and times and half of the time,' he signaled that the things of the Antichrist are for three-and-a-half years. For he says a time is one year, but times are two years, and half of a time is half of one year. These are the one thousand two hundred ninety days which Daniel foretold. 'And so, after the dispersion of the Jews happens, the suffering of the people is consummated, in those days the Antichrist is near, then they shall know all these things.'"** [58]

And in what appears to be a different document Hippolytus also wrote:

> "Thus, then, does the prophet set forth these things concerning the Antichrist, who shall be shameless, a war-maker, and despot, who, exalting himself above all kings and above every god, shall build the city of Jerusalem, and restore the sanctuary. Him the impious will worship as God, and will bend to him the knee, thinking him to be the Christ. He shall cut off the two witnesses and forerunners of Christ, who proclaim His glorious kingdom from heaven, as it is said: 'And I will give (power) unto my two witnesses, and they shall prophesy a thousand two hundred and threescore days,

---

58   Ibid, book 4, 56.5-57.1.

clothed in sackcloth.' **As also it was announced to Daniel: 'And one week shall confirm a covenant with many; and in the midst of the week it shall be that the sacrifice and oblation shall be removed"** —that the one week might be shown to be divided into two. The two witnesses, then, shall preach three years and a half; and Antichrist shall make war upon the saints during the rest of the week, and desolate the world, that what is written may be fulfilled: "And they shall make the abomination of desolation for a thousand two hundred and ninety days.'"** [59]

Hippolytus further said:

"With respect, then, to the particular judgment in the torments that are to come upon it in the last times by the hand of the tyrants who shall arise then, the clearest statement has been given in these passages. But it becomes us further diligently to examine and set forth the period at which these things shall come to pass, and how the little horn shall spring up in their midst. For when the legs of iron have issued in the feet and toes, according to the similitude of the image and that of the terrible beast, as has been shown in the above, (then shall be the time) when the iron and the clay shall be mingled together. **Now Daniel will set forth this subject to us. For he says, "And one week will make a covenant with many, and it shall be that in the midst (half) of the week my sacrifice and oblation shall cease." By one week, therefore, he meant the last week which is to be at the end of the whole world of which week the two prophets Enoch and Elias will take up the half. For they will preach 1, 260 days clothed in sackcloth, proclaiming repentance to the people and to all the nations."** [60]

59 "The interpretation by Hippolytus, (bishop) of Rome, of the visions of Daniel and Nebuchadnezzar, taken in conjunction," by Hippolytus, from paragraph 2 of "On Daniel," in "The Early Church Fathers: Ante-Nicene Fathers," vol. 5, ed. by Alexander Roberts and James Donaldson, as found in its American edition ed. by A. Cleveland Coxe.

60 "Treatise on Christ and Antichrist," by Hippolytus, paragraph 43, from "The Early Church Fathers: Ante-Nicene Fathers," vol. 5, ed. by Alexander Roberts and James Donaldson, as found in its American edition ed. by A. Cleveland Coxe.

Here we need to particularly notice the words. "By one week, therefore, he meant the last week which is to be at the end of the whole world of which week the two prophets Enoch and Elias will take up the half."

And in the same document, Hippolytus also wrote:

> "**For John says, 'And I will give power unto my two witnesses, and they shall prophesy a thousand two hundred and three-score days, clothed in sackcloth.' That is the half of the week whereof Daniel spake.** 'These are the two olive trees and the two candlesticks standing before the Lord of the earth. And if any man will hurt them, fire will proceed out of their mouth, and devour their enemies; and if any man will hurt them, he must in this manner be killed. These have power to shut heaven, that it rain not in the days of their prophecy; and have power over waters, to turn them to blood, and to smite the earth with all plagues as often as they will. And when they shall have finished their course and their testimony,' what saith the prophet? 'the beast that ascendeth out of the bottomless pit shall make war against them, and shall overcome them, and kill them,' because they will not give glory to Antichrist. For this is meant by the little horn that grows up. He, being now elated in heart, begins to exalt himself, and to glorify himself as God, persecuting the saints and blaspheming Christ, even as Daniel says, 'I considered the horn, and, behold, in the horn were eyes like the eyes of man, and a mouth speaking great things; and he opened his mouth to blaspheme God. And that born made war against the saints, and prevailed against them until the beast was slain, and perished, and his body was given to be burned.'" [61]

Hippolytus wrote further on this as follows:

> "**These things, then, being to come to pass, beloved, and the one week being divided into two parts, and the abomination of desolation being manifested then, and the two prophets**

---

61   Ibid, paragraph 47.

and forerunners of the Lord having finished their course, and the whole world finally approaching the consummation, what remains but the coming of our Lord and Saviour Jesus Christ from heaven, for whom we have looked in hope? who shall bring the conflagration and just judgment upon all who have refused to believe on Him. For the Lord says, 'And when these things begin to come to pass, then look up, and lift up your heads; for your redemption draweth nigh.' 'And there shall not a hair of your head perish.' 'For as the lightning cometh out of the east, and shineth even unto the west, so shall also the coming of the Son of man be. For wheresoever the carcase is, there will the eagles be gathered together.' Now the fall took place in paradise; for Adam fell there. And He says again, 'Then shall the Son of man send His angels, and they shall gather together His elect from the four winds of heaven.' And David also, in announcing prophetically the judgment and coming of the Lord, says, 'His going forth is from the end of the heaven, and His circuit unto the end of the heaven: and there is no one hid from the heat thereof.' By the heat he means the conflagration. And Esaias speaks thus: 'Come, my people, enter thou into thy chamber, (and) shut thy door: hide thyself as it were for a little moment, until the indignation of the Lord be overpast.' And Paul in like manner: 'For the wrath of God is revealed from heaven against all ungodliness and unrighteousness of men, who hold the truth of God in unrighteousness.'" [62]

Here, Hippolytus clearly taught that the seventieth week would be just before Christ comes to judge the world.

We now come to a few ancient documents attributed to Hippolytus, but which may have actually been penned by a different writer. For our purposes, it makes no difference who the writer actually was, for our only point is to demonstrate that these things were being taught in the church during that time period.

---

62   Ibid, paragraph 64.

The first of these is:

> **"For when Daniel said, 'I shall make my covenant for one week,' he indicated seven years; and the one half of the week is for the preaching of the prophets, and for the other half of the week—that is to say, for three years and a half—Antichrist will reign upon the earth.**
>
> And after this his kingdom and his glory shall be taken away. Behold, ye who love God, what manner of tribulation there shall rise in those days, such as has not been from the foundation of the world, no, nor ever shall be, except in those days alone. Then the lawless one, being lifted up in heart, will gather together his demons in man's form, and will abominate those who call him to the kingdom, and will pollute many souls."[63]

This writer again explicitly wrote that this week applies to the future in words almost identical to those we have already examined:

> **"As these things, therefore, of which we have spoken before are in the future, beloved, when the one week is divided into parts, and the abomination of desolation has arisen then, and the forerunners of the Lord have finished their proper course, and the whole world, in fine, comes to the consummation, what remains but the manifestation of our Lord and Saviour Jesus Christ, the Son of God, from heaven,** for whom we have hoped; who shall bring forth fire and all just judgment against those who have refused to believe in Him? For the Lord says, 'For as the lightning cometh out of the east, and shineth even unto the west, so shall also the coming of the Son of man be; for wheresoever the carcase is, there will the eagles be gathered together.' For the sign of the cross shall arise from the east even unto the west, in brightness exceeding that of the sun, and shall

63 "A discourse by the most blessed Hippolytus, bishop and martyr, on the end of the world, and on Antichrist, and on the second coming of our lord Jesus Christ." alleged to be by Hippolytus, paragraph 25, from "Appendix to the Works of Hippolytus, Containing Dubious and Spurious Pieces" in "The Early Church Fathers: Ante-Nicene Fathers," vol. 5, ed. by Alexander Roberts and James Donaldson, as found in its American edition ed. by A. Cleveland Coxe.

announce the advent and manifestation of the Judge, to give to every one according to his works. For concerning the general resurrection and the kingdom of the saints, Daniel says: 'And many of them that sleep in the dust of the earth shall awake, some to everlasting life, and some to shame and everlasting contempt.' And Isaiah says: 'The dead shall rise, and those in the tombs shall awake, and those in the earth shall rejoice.' And our Lord says: 'Many in that day shall hear the voice of the Son of God, and they that hear shall live.'" [64]

And this or a different writer again penned words almost identical to those of Hippolytus above, writing:

"For through the Scriptures we are instructed in two advents of the Christ and Saviour. And the first after the flesh was in humiliation, because He was manifested in lowly estate. So then His second advent is declared to be in glory; for He comes from heaven with power, and angels, and the glory of His Father. His first advent had John the Baptist as its forerun-her; and His second, in which He is to come in glory, will exhibit Enoch, and Elias, and John the Divine. Behold, too, the Lord's kindness to man; how even in the last times He shows His care for mortals, and pities them. For He will not leave us even then without prophets, but will send them to us for our instruction and assurance, and to make us give heed to the advent of the adversary, **as He intimated also of old in this Daniel. For he says, "I shall make a covenant of one week, and in the midst of the week my sacrifice and libation will be removed." For by one week he indicates the showing forth of the seven years which shall be in the last times. And the half of the week the two prophets, along with John, will take for the purpose of proclaiming to all the world the advent of Antichrist, that is to say, for a "thousand two hundred and sixty days clothed in sackcloth; " and they will work signs and wonders with the object of making men ashamed and repentant, even by these means, on account**

64 Ibid, paragraph 36.

of their surpassing lawlessness and impiety. "And if any man will hurt them, fire will proceed out of their mouth, and devour their enemies. These have power to shut heaven, that it rain not in the days of the advent of Antichrist, and to turn waters into blood, and to smite the earth with all plagues as often as they will." And when they have proclaimed all these things they will fall on the sword, cut off by the accuser. And they will fulfil their testimony, as Daniel also says; for he foresaw that the beast that came up out of the abyss would make war with them, namely with Enoch, Elias, and John, and would overcome them, and kill them, because of their refusal to give glory to the accuser. that is the little horn that sprang up. And he, being lifted up in heart, begins in the end to, exalt himself and glorify himself as God, persecuting the saints and blaspheming Christ." [65]

And we find the following, also credited to Hippolytus:

"And at first, indeed, that deceitful and lawless one, with crafty deceitfulness, will refuse such glory; but the men persisting, and holding by him, will declare him king. And thereafter he will be lifted up in heart, and he who was formerly gentle will become violent, and he who pursued love will become pitiless, and the humble in heart will become haughty and inhuman, and the hater of unrighteousness will persecute the righteous. Then, when he is elevated to his kingdom, he will marshal war; and in his wrath he will smite three mighty kings,—those, namely, of Egypt, Libya, and Ethiopia. And after that he will build the temple in Jerusalem, and will restore it again speedily, and give it over to the Jews. And then he will be lifted up in heart against every man; yea, he will speak blasphemy also against God, thinking in his deceit that he shall be king upon the earth hereafter for ever; not knowing, miserable wretch, that his kingdom is to be quickly brought to nought, and that he will quickly have to

---

65 "Appendix to the works of Hippolytus," by Hippolytus, section 21, from "The Early Church Fathers: Ante-Nicene Fathers," vol. 5, ed. by Alexander Roberts and James Donaldson, as found in its American edition ed. by A. Cleveland Coxe.

meet the fire which is prepared for him, along with all who trust him and serve him. **For when Daniel said, 'I shall make my covenant for one week,' he indicated seven years; and the one half of the week is for the preaching of the prophets, and for the other half of the week—that is to say, for three years and a half—Antichrist will reign upon the earth. And after this his kingdom and his glory shall be taken away.** Behold, ye who love God, what manner of tribulation there shall rise in those days, such as has not been from the foundation of the world, no, nor ever shall be, except in those days alone. Then the lawless one, being lifted up in heart, will gather together his demons in man's form, and will abominate those who call him to the kingdom, and will pollute many souls." [66]

And again, in another passage almost identical to two previous passages, we read:

> **"As these things, therefore, of which we have spoken before are in the future, beloved, when the one week is divided into parts, and the abomination of desolation has arisen then, and the forerunners of the Lord have finished their proper course, and the whole world, in fine, comes to the consummation, what remains but the manifestation of our Lord and Saviour Jesus Christ, the Son of God, from heaven,** for whom we have hoped; who shall bring forth fire and all just judgment against those who have refused to believe in Him? For the Lord says, 'For as the lightning cometh out of the east, and shineth even unto the west, so shall also the coming of the Son of man be; for wheresoever the carcase is, there will the eagles be gathered together.'" [67]

The fact that these passages are so highly similar to those known to have actually been penned by Hippolytus, suggests that these were fraudulent documents whose writer was pretending that his document was the work of

---

66 Ibid, section 25.

67 Ibid, section 36.

Hippolytus. But another possibility is that they are actually just highly edited versions of what Hippolytus wrote.

Next we come to Apollinarius of Laodicea. We do not know when he wrote this. But as he is believed to have lived from around A.D. 315 to A.D. 390. So the following is clearly from the mid to late fourth century. According to Jerome, this is a "word for word" translation of what Apollinarius said regarding the seventy weeks:

"To the period of four hundred and ninety years the wicked deeds are to be confined as well as all the crimes which shall ensue from those deeds. After these shall come the times of blessing, and the world is to be reconciled unto God at the advent of Christ, His Son. For from the coming forth of the Word, when Christ was born of the Virgin Mary, to the forty-ninth year, that is, the end of the seven weeks, [God] waited for Israel to repent. Thereafter, indeed, from the eighth year of Claudius Caesar [i.e., 48 A.D.] onward, the Romans took up arms against the Jews. For it was in His thirtieth year, according to the Evangelist Luke, that the Lord incarnate began His preaching of the Gospel (Luke 1) [sic!]. According to the Evangelist John (John 2 and 11), Christ completed two years over a period of three passovers. The years of Tiberius' reign from that point onward are to be reckoned at six; then there were the four years of the reign of Gaius Caesar, surnamed Caligula, and eight more years in the reign of Claudius. This makes a total of forty-nine years, or the equivalent of seven weeks of years. But when four hundred thirty-four years shall have elapsed after that date, that is to say, the sixty-two weeks, then [i.e. in 482 A.D.] **Jerusalem and the Temple shall be rebuilt during three and a half years within the final week, beginning with the advent of Elias, who according to the dictum of our Lord and Savior (Luke 1) [sic!] is going to come and turn back the hearts of the fathers towards their children. And then the Antichrist shall come,** and according to the Apostle [reading apostolum for apostolorum] he is going to sit in the temple of God (II Thess. 2) and be slain by the breath of our Lord and Savior after he has waged war against the saints. And thus it shall come to pass that the middle of the week shall mark the confirmation of God's covenant with the saints, and the middle of the week in turn shall mark the issuing of the decree under the authority of Antichrist that no more sacrifices be offered. For the Antichrist shall set up the abomination of desolation, that is, an idol or statue of his own god, within the Temple. Then shall ensue the final devastation and the condemnation of the Jewish people, who after their rejection of Christ's truth shall embrace the lie of the Antichrist." [68]

We need to notice here the words, said concerning the seventy weeks, that "After these shall come the times of blessing, and the world is to be reconciled unto God at the advent of Christ, His Son." and "Jerusalem and the Temple shall be rebuilt during three and a half years within the final week." So, although he placed the entire seventy weeks after the time of Christ, Apollinarius clearly taught that the seventieth week would take place just before the return of Christ.

Jerome himself, who published this translation (into Latin,) declined to give his opinion on this passage, saying, "I realize that this question has been argued over in various ways by men of greatest learning, and that each of them has expressed his views according to the capacity of his own genius. And so, because it is unsafe to pass judgment upon the opinions of the great teachers of the Church and to set one above another, I shall simply repeat the view of each, and leave it to the reader's judgment as to whose explanation ought to be followed" (pg. 95 in the volume cited).

He then went on to summarize the views of many who commented on this, but omitting Irenaeus. In addition to the translation above, he summarized the views of Hippolytus, (pp. 103-104) and of Eusebius, (pp. 98-103) Clement of Alexandria, (p. 105) Origen, (pp. 105-106) and

---

68   Jerome's translation of the comments of Apollinarius of Laodicea on the seventy weeks, as found in "Jerome's Commentary on Daniel," by Jerome, pp. 104-105, translated by Gleason L. Archer, Jr., pub. by Baker Book House, Grand Rapids, 1958.

Tertullian, (pp. 106-108) all of which except Hippolytus interpreted the seventieth week to be already fulfilled. He also gave he views of "the Hebrews," (pp. 108-110) and included what he claimed was a **"verbatim"** translation of the comments on the subject by Julius Africanus, whose views we will now examine.

Jerome said, "**Moreover this same Apollinarius asserts that he conceived this idea about the proper dating from the fact that Africanus, (p. 549) the author of the Tempora [Chronology], whose explanation I have inserted above, affirms that the final week will occur at the end of the world. Yet, says Apollinarius, it is impossible that periods so linked together be wrenched apart, but rather the time-segments must all be joined together in conformity with Daniel's prophecy.**"[69]

So according to Jerome, Julius Africanus was an ancient writer who taught that Daniel's seventieth week had not been fulfilled, even though this conclusion appears to contradict his own translation of those writings, as will be seen below.

Regardless of that problem, the comments of Julius Africanus are still significant to this examination because, like modern Dispensationalists, he taught the concept of calculating the seventy weeks on the basis of "**Hebrew years.**"

The following is from "The Chronography of Julius Africanus." As this chronography ended with the year A.D. 221, it appears that this was the year it was finished.

> "**It is by calculating from Artaxerxes, therefore, up to the time of Christ that the seventy weeks are made up, according to the numeration of the Jews**. For from Nehemiah, who was despatched by Artaxerxes to build Jerusalem in the 115th year of the Persian empire, and the 4th year of the 83d Olympiad, and the 20th year of the reign of Artaxerxes himself, up to ibis date,

---

69 Ibid, pg. 105

which was the second year of the 202d Olympiad, and the 16th year of the reign of Tiberius Caesar, **there are reckoned 475 years, which make 490 according to the Hebrew numeration, as they measure the years by the course of the moon; so that, as is easy to show, their year consists of 354 days, while the solar year has 3651/4days. For the latter exceeds the period of twelve months, according to the moon's course, by 111/4 days. Hence the Greeks and the Jews insert three intercalary months every 8 years. For 8 times 111/4 days makes up 3 months. Therefore 475 years make 59 periods of 8 years each, and 3 months be-sides. But since thus there are 3 intercalary months every 8 years, we get thus 15 years minus a few days; and these being added to the 475 years, make up in all the 70 weeks."** [70]

And again, Julius Africanus wrote similarly:

"As to His works severally, and His cures effected upon body and soul, and the mysteries of His doctrine, and the resurrection from the dead, these have been most authoritatively set forth by His disciples and apostles before us. On the whole world there pressed a most fearful darkness; and the rocks were rent by an earthquake, and many places in Judea and other districts were thrown down. This darkness Thallus, in the third book of his History, calls, as appears to me without reason, an eclipse of the sun. For the Hebrews celebrate the passover on the 14th day according to the moon, and the passion of our Saviour fails on the day before the passover; but an eclipse of the sun takes place only when the moon comes under the sun. And it cannot happen at any other time but in the interval between the first day of the new moon and the last of the old, that is, at their junction: how then should an eclipse be supposed to happen when the moon is almost diametrically opposite the sun? Let that opinion pass however;

---

70 "The Extant Fragments of the Five Books of the Chronography of Julius Africanus," by Julius Africanus, part 16, "On the Seventy Weeks of Daniel," from "The Early Church Fathers: Ante-Nicene Fathers," vol. 6, ed. by Alexander Roberts and James Donaldson, as found in its American edition ed. by A. Cleveland Coxe.

let it carry the majority with it; and let this portent of the world be deemed an eclipse of the sun, like others a portent only to the eye. Phlegon records that, in the time of Tiberius Caesar, at full moon, there was a full eclipse of the sun from the sixth hour to the ninth—manifestly that one of which we speak. But what has an eclipse in common with an earthquake, the rending rocks, and the resurrection of the dead, and so great a perturbation throughout the universe? Surely no such event as this is recorded for a long period. But it was a darkness induced by God, because the Lord happened then to suffer. And calculation makes out that the period of 70 weeks, as noted in Daniel, is completed at this time.

"From Artaxerxes, moreover, 70 weeks are reckoned up to the time of Christ, according to the numeration of the Jews. For from Nehemiah, who was sent by Artaxerxes to people Jerusalem, about the 120th year of the Persian empire, and in the 20th year of Artaxerxes himself, and the 4th year of the 83d Olympiad, up to this time, which was the 2d year of the 102d Olympiad, and the 16th year of the reign of Tiberius Caesar, there are given 475 years, which make 490 Hebrew years, since they measure the years by the lunar month of 29 ½ days, as may easily be explained, the annual period according to the sun consisting of 365 1/4 days, while the lunar period of 12 months has 11 1/4 days less. For which reason the Greeks and the Jews insert three intercalary months every eight years. For 8 times 11 1/4 days make 3 months. The 475 years, therefore, contain 59 periods of 8 years and three months over: thus, the three intercalary months for every 8 years being added, we get 15 years, and these together with the 475 years make 70 weeks. Let no one now think us unskilled in the calculations of astronomy, when we fix without further ado the number of days at 365 1/4. For it is not in ignorance of the truth, but rather by reason of exact study, that we have stated our opinion so shortly. But let what follows also be presented as in outline to those who endeavour to inquire minutely into all things.

"Each year in the general consists of 365 days; and the space of a day and night being divided into nineteen parts, we have also five of these. And in saying that the year consists of 365 1/4 days, and there being the five nineteenth parts ... to the 475 there are 6 1/4 days. Furthermore, we find, according to exact computation, that the lunar month has 29 ½ days.... And these come to a little time. **Now it happens that from the 20th year of the reign of Artaxerxes (as it is given in Ezra among the Hebrews), which, according to the Greeks, was the 4th year of the 80th Olympiad, to the 16th year of Tiberius Caesar, which was the second year of the 102d Olympiad, there are in all the 475 years already noted, which in the Hebrew system make 490 years, as has been previously stated, that is, 70 weeks, by which period the time of Christ's advent was measured in the announcement made to Daniel by Gabriel. And if any one thinks that the 15 Hebrew years added to the others involve us in an error of 10, nothing at least which cannot be accounted for has been introduced. And the 1 ½ week which we suppose must be added to make the whole number, meets the question about the 15 years, and removes the difficulty about the time; and that the prophecies are usually put forth in a somewhat symbolic form, is quite evident.**" [71]

As a side note, we must notice that two errors are introduced into this calculation. The first is seen in the words "**from Nehemiah, who was sent by Artaxerxes to people Jerusalem, about the 120th year of the Persian empire.**" This is a logical error, for exact calculations leave no room for "abouts." And we find the second at the end, when he said that "**the 1 ½ week which we suppose must be added to make the whole number, meets the question.**" This is a spiritual error, for he presumes to minimize the exact nature of the numbers in the prophecy. He then made an excuse for this by saying, "**and that the prophecies are usually put forth in a somewhat symbolic form, is quite evident.**"

---

71   Ibid, part 18.

Again, Jerome gave his translation of a portion of this work, saying, "Africanus has this to say concerning the seventy weeks (and I quote him verbatim)."

"The chapter which we read in Daniel concerning the seventy weeks contains many remarkable details, which require too lengthy a discussion at this point; and so we must discuss only what pertains to our present task, namely that which concerns chronology. There is no doubt but what it constitutes a prediction of Christ's advent, for He appeared to the world at the end of seventy weeks. After Him the crimes were consummated and sin reached its end and iniquity was destroyed. An eternal righteousness also was proclaimed which overcame the mere righteousness of the law; and the vision and the prophecy were fulfilled, inasmuch as the Law and the Prophets endured until the time of John the Baptist (Luke 16), and then the Saint of saints was anointed. And all these things were the objects of hope, prior to Christ's incarnation, rather than the objects of actual possession. Now the angel himself specified seventy weeks of years, that is to say, four hundred and ninety years from the issuing of the word that the petition be granted and that Jerusalem be rebuilt. The specified interval began in the twentieth year of Artaxerxes, King of the Persians; for it was his cupbearer, Nehemiah (Neh. 1), who, as we read in the book of Ezra, petitioned the king and obtained his request that Jerusalem be rebuilt. And this was the word, or decree, which granted permission for the construction of the city and its encompassment with walls; for up until that time it had lain open to the incursions of the surrounding nations. But if one points to the command of King Cyrus, who granted to all who desired it permission to return to Jerusalem, the fact of the matter is that the high priest Jesus and Zerubbabel, and later on the priest Ezra, together with the others who had been willing to set forth from Babylon with them, only made an abortive attempt to construct the Temple and the city with its walls, but were prevented by the surrounding nations from completing the task, on the pretext that the king had not so ordered. And thus the work remained incomplete until Nehemiah's time and the twentieth year of King Artaxerxes. Hence the captivity lasted for seventy years prior to the Persian rule. At this period in the Persian Empire a hundred and fifteen years had elapsed since its inception, but it was the one hundred and eighty-fifth year from the captivity of Jerusalem when Artaxerxes first gave orders for the walls of Jerusalem to be built. Nehemiah was in charge of this undertaking, and the street was built and the surrounding walls were erected. Now if you compute seventy weeks of years from that date, you can come out to the time of Christ. But if we wish to take any other date as the starting point for these weeks, then the dates will show a discrepancy and we shall encounter many difficulties. For if the seventy weeks are computed from the time of Cyrus and his decree of indulgence which effectuated the release of the Jewish captives, then we shall encounter a deficit of a hundred years and more short of the stated number of seventy weeks. If we reckon from the day when the angel spoke to Daniel, the deficit would be much greater An even greater number of years is added, if you wish to put the beginning of the weeks at the commencement of the captivity. For the kingdom of the Persians endured for two hundred and thirty years until the rise of the Macedonian kingdom; then the Macedonians themselves reigned for three hundred years. From that date until the sixteenth year of Tiberius Caesar, when Christ suffered death, is an interval of sixty [sic!] years. All of these years added together come to the number of five hundred and ninety, with the result that a hundred years remain to be accounted for. **On the other hand, the interval from the twentieth year of Artaxerxes to the time of Christ completes the figure of seventy weeks, if we reckon according to the lunar computation of the Hebrews, who did not number their months according to the movement of the sun, but rather according to the moon. For the interval from the one hundred fiftieth year of the Persian Empire, when Artaxerxes, as king thereof, attained the twentieth year of his reign (and this was the fourth year of the eighty-third Olympiad), up until the two hundred and second Olympiad (for it was the second year of** that Olympiad which was the fifteenth year of Tiberius Caesar) comes out to be the grand total of four hundred seventy-five years. This would result in four hundred ninety Hebrew years, reckoning according to the lunar months as we have suggested. For according to their computation, these years can be made up of months of twenty-nine and a half days each. This means that the sun, during a period of four hundred ninety years, completes its revolution in three hundred sixty-five days and a quarter, and this amounts to twelve lunar months for each individual year, with eleven and a fourth days left over to spare. Consequently the Greeks and Jews over a period of eight years insert three intercalary months (*embolimoi*). For if you will multiply eleven and a quarter days by eight, you will come out to ninety days, which equal three months. Now if you divide the eight-year periods into four hundred seventy-five years, your quotient will be fifty-nine plus three months. These fifty-nine plus eight-year periods produce enough intercalary months to make up fifteen years, more or less; and if you will add these fifteen years to the four hundred seventy-five years, you will come out to seventy weeks of years, that is, a total of four hundred and ninety years." [72]

So it is very clear that the doctrine that the seventieth week of Daniel's prophecy remains to be fulfilled in the future is not a new idea at all. For we have seen that this concept was clearly taught in some of the very oldest surviving Christian writings on the subject, and was still being taught at least until the mid fourth century. And was advanced as a possibility even as late as the fifth century. We have also seen that the concept of calculating these seventy weeks (490 years) on the basis of **"Hebrew years"** was also being taught in ancient times.

---

72   Jerome's translation of an extract from the "Chronography," by Julius Africanus, as found in "Jerome's Commentary on Daniel," by Jerome, pp. 95-98, translated by Gleason L. Archer, Jr., pub. by Baker Book House, Grand Rapids, 1958.

CHAPTER 6

Ancient Teaching of a Rapture
Before the Great Tribulation

It has been widely claimed that the doctrine of a rapture before the tribulation could not be correct because it had never been taught before the 1800s. And these people contend that anything the church never taught in its first eighteen centuries, could not be correct.

This is false on two fronts. First, we read **"I have more understanding than all my teachers: for thy testimonies are my meditation"** (Psalm 119:99). This, actually, should be true of every generation, for when we have learned everything our teachers can teach us, our studies are not completed. Rather, our real studies are just now ready to begin. For we start with the knowledge set before us, and build up from there, using meditation upon God's testimonies. So whoever first taught a given doctrine, or how long it has been taught, are immaterial. The only thing that counts is whether or not the scriptures actually teach it.

But this claim has another error. And that is that it simply is not correct. On page 178 of his book, "Dispensationalism before Darby." William C. Watson listed about two dozen writers who, in the 1600s and 1700s, taught a rapture significantly before the Lord returns to judge the world for its wickedness. But all of these were late comers. For the doctrine of a rapture before the great tribulation was taught, and sometimes very clearly taught, in ancient times, as we shall see in this chapter.

We need to be aware of one detail to actually understand the following quotations from these ancient writers, and why they were actually teaching a rapture before the great tribulation, even though their writings included comments about "the church" suffering persecution under the Antichrist.

If we carefully examine all their writings, they always give the time of the Antichrist as three and a half years, which they call the "great tribulation," as you will see below. This writer has not found even one exception to this rule. These same ancients clearly taught that Daniel's seventieth week remains to be fulfilled in the future. But they only foresaw the great tribulation as the last half of this week. So, as will become evident below, they only taught that the tribulation would last three and a half years, or a half week, instead of seven years, as is commonly taught today. Thus, from their viewpoint, their position was truly pre-tribulational, because they taught a rapture before the "great tribulation." But what they taught was actually what today would be called a mid-tribulation rapture.

The very oldest Christian commentary on Bible prophecy of any significant length that has survived to our day is the last twelve chapters of "Against Heresies," by Irenaeus. (There were older such commentaries, but all of them were either only short comments in discussions about other subjects, or have been lost.) This is thought to have been published between the years A.D. 186 and 188, and says:

> "Those nations however, who did not of themselves raise up their eyes unto heaven, nor returned thanks to their Maker, nor wished to behold the light of truth, but who were like blind mice concealed in the depths of ignorance, the word justly reckons 'as waste water from a sink, and as the turning-weight of a balance—in fact, as nothing;' so far useful and serviceable to

the just, as stubble conduces towards the growth of the wheat, and its straw, by means of combustion, serves for working gold. **And therefore, when in the end the Church shall be suddenly caught up from this, it is said, 'There shall be tribulation such as has not been since the beginning, neither shall be.' For this is the last contest of the righteous, in which, when they overcome they are crowned with incorruption."** ("Against Heresies," by Irenaeus, Book V, chapter 29, paragraph 1.)

Here we find a clear teaching of a pre-tribulation rapture. But Irenaeus also wrote:

"For all these and other words were unquestionably spoken in reference to the resurrection of the just, which takes place after the coming of Antichrist, and the destruction of all nations under his rule;" ("Against Heresies," by Irenaeus, Book V, chapter 35, paragraph 1.)

Here we see this same ancient writer just as explicitly saying that "**the resurrection of the just**" "**takes place after the coming of Antichrist.**" On the surface, this would seem to flatly contradict his other statement. But this is not the case. First, we need to notice that Irenaeus did not say that "**the resurrection of the just**" takes place after the reign of Antichrist. He only said it "**takes place after the coming of Antichrist, and the destruction of all nations under his rule.**" To see the significance of this, we need to consider another statement from this same ancient document:

"**But when this Antichrist shall have devastated all things in this world, he will reign for three years and six months**, and sit in the temple at Jerusalem; and then the Lord will come from heaven in the clouds, in the glory of the Father, sending this man and those who follow him into the lake of fire; but bringing in for **the righteous** the times of the kingdom." ("Against Heresies," by Irenaeus, Book V, chapter 30, paragraph 4.)

Here we find first, a distinct statement that Antichrist would reign for three years and six months, but also a distinct statement that this three years and six months would be after **"this Antichrist shall have devastated all things in this world."** Thus we see that Irenaeus placing **"the resurrection of the just"** **"after the coming of Antichrist, and the destruction of all nations under his rule,"** was not saying the rapture would be after the three and a half year reign of Antichrist. Rather, he placed the rapture at the beginning of that three and a half year reign. That is, he was saying that the time of **"tribulation such as has not been since the beginning, neither shall be"** was the three and a half year reign of Antichrist.

Irenaeus very clearly put the church in at least the first part of the time of Antichrist, as we can see in the following:

> "'And the ten horns which thou sawest are ten kings, who have received no kingdom as yet, but shall receive power as if kings one hour with the beast. These have one mind, and give their strength and power to the beast. These shall make war with the Lamb, and the Lamb shall overcome them, because He is the Lord of lords and the King of kings.' It is manifest, therefore, that of these [potentates], he who is to come shall slay three, and subject the remainder to his power, and that he shall be himself the eighth among them. **And they shall lay Babylon waste, and burn her with fire, and shall give their kingdom to the beast, and put the Church to flight.** After that they shall be destroyed by the coming of our Lord." ("Against Heresies," by Irenaeus, Book V, chapter 26, paragraph 1.)

This is the only place Irenaeus used the word **"church"** in regard to these events, other than the place where he explicitly said **"the Church shall be suddenly caught up"** before the **"tribulation such as has not been since the beginning, neither shall be."** But he used the word **"we,"** which certainly seems to have the same meaning, here:

"But he indicates the number of the name now, **that when this man comes we may avoid him,** being aware who he is: the name, however, is suppressed, because it is not worthy of being proclaimed by the Holy Spirit." ("Against Heresies," by Irenaeus, Book V, chapter 26, paragraph 1.)

These last two statements make it very clear that Irenaeus placed the rapture at least after "**the coming of Antichrist**." We have already noticed that in statements about events before the three and a half year reign of Antichrist, he used the words "**the church**" and "**we**." But in his statements about persecutions during the three and a half year reign of Antichrist, he changed this terminology. We remember that in his statement about the church being "**suddenly caught up,**" he called the tribulation "**the last contest of the righteous, in which, when they overcome they are crowned with incorruption**." He used the term "**the righteous**" again when he spoke of the faithful in that time in this statement:

> "For that image which was set up by Nebuchadnezzar had indeed a height of sixty cubits, while the breadth was six cubits; on account of which Ananias, Azarias, and Misaël, when they did not worship it, were cast into a furnace of fire, **pointing out prophetically, by what happened to them, the wrath against the righteous which shall arise towards the [time of the] end.** For that image, taken as a whole, was a prefiguring of this man's coming, decreeing that he should undoubtedly himself alone be worshipped by all men." ("Against Heresies," by Irenaeus, Book V, chapter 29, paragraph 2.)

We remember that Irenaeus used this same term in speaking of the beginning of the kingdom, saying, "**bringing in for the righteous the times of the kingdom**." He also used a second term for these faithful ones during that time, calling them "**saints**" in the following statements:

"Daniel too, looking forward to the end of the last kingdom, i.e., the ten last kings, amongst whom the kingdom of those men shall be partitioned, and upon whom the son of perdition shall come, declares that ten horns shall spring from the beast, and that another little horn shall arise in the midst of them, and that three of the former shall be rooted up before his face. He says: 'And, behold, eyes were in this horn as the eyes of a man, and a mouth speaking great things, and his look was more stout than his fellows. I was looking, and this horn made war against **the saints**, and prevailed against them, until the Ancient of days came and gave judgment to **the saints of the most high God**, and the time came, and **the saints** obtained the kingdom.' Then, further on, in the interpretation of the vision, there was said to him: 'The fourth beast shall be the fourth kingdom upon earth, which shall excel all other kingdoms, and devour the whole earth, and tread it down, and cut it in pieces. And its ten horns are ten kings which shall arise; and after them shall arise another, who shall surpass in evil deeds all that were before him, and shall overthrow three kings; and he shall speak words against the most high God, and wear out **the saints of the most high God**, and shall purpose to change times and laws; and [everything] shall be given into his hand until a time of times and a half time,' that is, for three years and six months, during which time, when he comes, he shall reign over the earth." ("Against Heresies," by Irenaeus, Book V, chapter 25, paragraph 3.)

"And then he points out the time that his tyranny shall last, during which **the saints** shall be put to flight, **they who offer a pure sacrifice unto God**: 'And in the midst of the week,' he says, 'the sacrifice and the libation shall be taken away, and the abomination of desolation [shall be brought] into the temple: even unto the consummation of the time shall the desolation be complete.' **Now three years and six months constitute the half-week.**" ("Against Heresies," by Irenaeus, Book V, chapter 25, paragraph 4.)

We need to notice that both of these statements are about the three and a half year reign of Antichrist, and thus speak of a time after Irenaeus placed the "**resurrection of the just**." And in these statements, he changed the words "**the church**," or "**we**," to "**the righteous**" or "**the saints**."

Why are the exact words Irenaeus used significant? Because a doctrine of a pre-tribulation rapture requires words like "**the church**" or "**we**" in statements about the godly during events up to and including the moment when "**the Church shall be suddenly caught up**." But when speaking of times after this, that is, after the rapture, the proper (and scriptural) terms for godly people are "**the righteous**" or "**saints**." Again, the doctrine requires a different term for those who are resurrected at the time of the rapture, for that resurrection includes Old Testament believers, who were thus not members of the church. And this is exactly what Irenaeus did, calling the resurrection by its scriptural name of "**the resurrection of the just**."

Now some will want to discount any claim that Irenaeus was intentionally using well selected terminology in these statements. But he used the same precision in his comments about recognizing the Antichrist when he appeared. For, as we have already noticed, when he was speaking of true believers he said "**But he indicates the number of the name now, that when this man comes we may avoid him**." But when he was speaking of men who might be deceived by the Antichrist, he systematically referred to them by using the words "**those**," "**these**," "**they**," and "**them**," as we see in the following statements:

> "Moreover, another danger, by no means trifling, shall overtake **those** who falsely presume that they know the name of Antichrist. For if **these** men assume one [number], when this [Antichrist] shall come having another, **they** will be easily led away by him, as supposing him not to be the expected one, who must be guarded against." ("Against Heresies," by Irenaeus, Book V, chapter 30, end of paragraph 1)

"**These** men, therefore, ought to learn [what really is the state of the case], and go back to the true number of the name, that **they** be not reckoned among false prophets. But, knowing the sure number declared by Scripture, that is, six hundred sixty and six, let **them** await, in the first place, the division of the kingdom into ten; then, in the next place, when these kings are reigning, and beginning to set their affairs in order, and advance their kingdom, [let them learn] to acknowledge that he who shall come claiming the kingdom for himself, and shall terrify **those** men of whom we have been speaking, having a name containing the aforesaid number, is truly the abomination of desolation." ("Against Heresies," by Irenaeus, Book V, chapter 30, beginning of paragraph 2.)

Thus we see that Irenaeus used precise terminology that clearly distinguished between these two groups. He again used the scriptural words "**those**," along with "**ye**" and "**he**," rather than his own words, when speaking of the need for the inhabitants of the land of Judea to flee when they see the abomination of desolation.

"But when **ye** shall see the abomination of desolation, which has been spoken of by Daniel the prophet, standing in the holy place (let him that readeth understand), then let **those** who are in Judea flee into the mountains; and **he** who is upon the house-top, let him not come down to take anything out of his house: for there shall then be great hardship, such as has not been from the beginning of the world until now, nor ever shall be." ("Against Heresies," by Irenaeus, Book V, chapter 25, paragraph 2.)

Finally, Irenaeus made one more statement that touches this matter, saying:

"Has the Word come for the ruin and for the resurrection of many? For the ruin, certainly, of **those who do not believe Him**, to whom also He has threatened a greater damnation in the judgment-day than that of Sodom and Gomorrah; but for the resurrection of **believers**, and **those** who do the will of His Father in heaven." (Against Heresies," by Irenaeus, Book V, chapter 27, paragraph 1.)

In this passage Irenaeus again changes the words "**the church**" to "**believers**," and calls them "**those**," rather than "**we**." And he implies a simultaneous judgment-day for unbelievers and resurrection of believers. Some will assume that this last dettail proves he was not saying that the rapture will be before the tribulation. But this is in full accord with the doctrine of the pre-tribulation rapture. For there will be people who turn to God during the time of the tribulation, and they will be persecuted and slain for their faith. But those who teach a pre-tribulation rapture hold that these "tribulation saints" are not part of the church. These will be resurrected at approximately the same time as when Christ comes in power and glory to judge the world. (The scriptures do not say their resurrection happens when He comes. But Revelation 20:4 says, "**they lived and reigned with Christ for a thousand years.**" So we know that their resurrection takes place at least at approximately the same time as He comes.)

So now we are faced with two choices. We can either assume that Irenaeus was exceedingly careless as to his wording, and simply did not mean what he said. Or we can assume that the precision of his wording was not a mere coincidence, but that he chose his exact words carefully and with intent. In that case, we are forced to conclude that Irenaeus meant exactly what he said when he wrote:

> **"And therefore, when in the end the Church shall be suddenly caught up from this, it is said, 'There shall be tribulation such as has not been since the beginning, neither shall be.'"**

We come now to Victorinus, [73] who is thought to have written his commentary on the Apocalypse (the Revelation) sometime around the year A.D. 240

Victorinus said concerning Revelation 6:14:

> "'And the heaven withdrew as a scroll that is rolled up.' For the heaven to be rolled way, **that is, that the Church shall be taken away.'** 'And the mountain and the islands were moved from their places." Mountains and islands removed from their places intimate that in the last persecution all men departed from their places; **that is, that the good will be removed, seeking to avoid the persecution."**

We need to notice here that Victorinus did not make these clauses active, saying "the church shall go away," or "the good will flee." Instead these clauses are both in the passive, that the church **"shall be taken away,"** and that the good **"will be removed."** So this is not, as some allege, a statement that the church will flee out of society, hiding in wilderness places.

Again, he said concerning Revelation 15:1:

> "'And I saw another great and wonderful sign, seven angels having the seven last plagues; for in them is completed the indignation of God.' For the wrath of God always strikes the obstinate people with seven plagues, that is, perfectly, as it is said in Leviticus; **and these shall be in the last time, when the Church shall have gone out of the midst."**

This, being in the active, could refer to flight. But when taken in connection to the previous statement, we see that this was not what Victorinus was saying.

---

73 All quotations of Victorinus in this book are from "In Apocalypsin," by Victorinus, as presented online by Biblicalia at http://www.bombaxo.com/blog/patristic-stuff/victorinus-in-apocalypsin/, and as also found online at http://www.preteristarchive.com/StudyArchive/v/victorinus-of-petau.html.

Some will protest that these are not truly the words of Victorinus. For they are different in the version presented in "The Early Church Fathers, Ante-Nicene Fathers," volume 7. These protestors think that Victorinus was Amillennial, and that thus his comments could not have contained these words. But these people are unaware that the copy reproduced in "the Early Church Fathers" is not the actual document written by Victorinus, but a rewritten version produced by Jerome. Jerome's own statement concerning his revision of this work is found in his letter to Anatolius, which is in the prologue to his revision of the Commentary on the Apocalypse by Victorinus. In this letter, Jerome said:

> "Those crossing over the perilous seas find different dangers. If a storm of winds has become violent, it is a terror; if the moderate air has calmed the back of the elements, lying calm, they fear traps. Thus is seen in this book which you have sent to me, which is seen to contain the explanation of the Apocalypse by Victorinus. Also, it is dangerous, and opens to the barkings of detractors, to judge the short works of eminent men. **For even earlier Papias, the bishop of Hierapolis, and Nepos, the bishop of parts of Egypt, perceived of the kingdom of the thousand years just as Victorinus.** And because you are in your letters entreating me, I do not want to delay, but nor do I want to scorn praying. I immediately unwound the books of the greats, and what I found in their commentaries about the kingdom of the thousand years, **I added to the little work of Victorinus, erasing from there those things which he perceived according to the letter.**
>
> "From the beginning of the book to the sign of the cross, we have corrected things which are the corruptions of inexperience of scribes. **Know that from there to the end of the book is added.** Now it is yours to judge, and to confirm what pleases. If our life will be made longer and the Lord will give health, for you, our most capable genius will sweat over this book, dearest Anatolius."

Both the original text by Victorinus, and the prologue by Jerome, can be read in their entirety at either of the websites listed in footnote 73 on page 98.

So Victorinus indeed taught "that the Church shall be taken away," and that "the good will be removed, seeking to avoid the persecution." And that in the last time "the church shall have gone out of the midst." This most certainly appears to be a teaching of a rapture before the great tribulation.

Again, there is an ancient sermon titled "On the Last Times, the Antichrist, and the End of the World." [74] Most of the surviving copies of this sermon say it was written by Ephraem, but one says its author was Isadore of Seville. Based on events the sermon said were impending, various scholars have estimated its date from as early as A.D. 373 to as late as A.D. 627. Paul J. Alexander gave what seems to be the most satisfactory analysis of its date, concluding that the original had to have been written in or near the fourth century, but that copiers had added other material sometime around the seventh century.[75] According to Alexander, two of the surviving copies of this sermon date from the mid to late eighth century and one has been dated to the eighth or ninth century. [76] As scholars do not believe the unknown author could have been the famous Ephraem the Syrian, (who is also known a Ephraem of Nisbis) they call the unknown author of this sermon, Pseudo-Ephraem. The sermon was divided into ten paragraphs, and said in paragraph 2:

> "Why therefore do we not reject every care of earthly actions and prepare ourselves for the meeting of the Lord Christ, so that he may draw us from the confusion, which overwhelms all the world? Believe you me, dearest brother, because the coming (advent) of the Lord is nigh, believe you me, because the end of the world is at hand, believe me, because it is the very last time. Or do you not believe unless you see with your eyes? See to it

74 Among modern prophecy teachers, this document was originally discovered by Grant Jeffrey, and then widely circulated by Thomas Ice.

75 "Byzantine Apocalyptic Tradition," by Paul J. Alexander, University of California Press, Berkeley, CA, 1985, pg. 137.

76 Ibid, same page.

that this sentence be not fulfilled among you of the prophet who declares: 'Woe to those who desire to see the day of the Lord!' **For all the saints and elect of God are gathered, prior to the tribulation that is to come, and are taken to the Lord lest they see the confusion that is to overwhelm the world because of our sins.**" [77]

It would be difficult to make a more clear statement of the doctrine of the pre-tribulation rapture. But even so, some still deny that it was pre-tribulational, because of an interpretation they put on paragraph 10 of the same sermon, which said:

"And when the three and a half years have been completed, the time of the Antichrist, through which he will have seduced the world, after the resurrection of the two prophets, in the hour which the world does not know, and on the day which the enemy of son of perdition does not know, will come the sign of the Son of Man, and coming forward the Lord shall appear with great power and much majesty, with the sign of the wood of salvation going before him, and also even with all the powers of the heavens with the whole chorus of the saints, with those who bear the sign of the holy cross upon their shoulders, as the angelic trumpet precedes him, which shall sound and declare: **Arise, O sleeping ones, arise, meet Christ, because his hour of judgment has come!** Then Christ shall come and the enemy shall be thrown into confusion, and the Lord shall destroy him by the spirit of his mouth."[78]

These people claim that the rapture is in this paragraph, instead of paragraph 2, because of the words "**Arise, O sleeping ones, arise, meet Christ,**

77 "On the Last Times, the Antichrist, and the End of the World," author unknown, but called pseudo-Ephraem, paragraph 2. As translated by Cameron Rhoades, instructor of Latin at Tyndale Theological Seminary, from C.P. Caspari, Briefe, Abhandlungen und Predigten aus den letzten zwei Jahrhunderten des kirchliche Alterthums und dem Anfang des Mittelaters (Christiania, 1890), pp. 208-20, which was cited by Alexander in footnote 2, pg. 137.
This translation is available online at: http://www.according2prophecy.org/lastimes.html.

78 Ibid, paragraph 10.

because his hour of judgment has come!" But this is a serious error. Are we to think this unknown writer was unfamiliar with John 5:24, where Jesus said, **"Most assuredly, I say to you, he who hears My word and believes in Him who sent Me has everlasting life, and shall not come into judgment, but has passed from death into life."** The **"hour of judgment"** is not for the saints of God. It is for sinners. These people would not have made this error if they had noticed who this paragraph says will be with the Lord as He comes. It is **"all the powers of the heavens with the whole chorus of the saints, with those who bear the sign of the holy cross upon their shoulders."** Thus we see the previously raptured saints of God coming with the Lord when He comes to judge the world. This was stated twice over, first calling them **"the whole chorus of the saints,"** and then **"those who bear the sign of the holy cross upon their shoulders."** It was completely consistent to have the rapture before **"the whole chorus of the saints"** coming with the Lord when He comes **"with great power and much majesty"** for **"his hour of judgement."**

Finally, these same people also claim that the sermon has the church still in the world at the time of the Antichrist, because the sermon also says, at the end of paragraph 8:

> "But **those who wander through the deserts, fleeing from the face of the serpent, bend their knees to God,** just as lambs to the adders of their mothers, being sustained by the salvation of the Lord, and while wandering in states of desertion, they eat herbs." [79]

But this argument is based on another error. These people interpret every reference to people turning to God to mean the church. But those who believe that the rapture will be before the tribulation have always taught that some will repent and turn to God after the church has been removed. We remember that Irenaeus had referred to these with the words that this

---

79 Ibed, paragraph 8.

tribulation "is the last contest of the righteous, in which, when they overcome they are crowned with incorruption." So the fact that the sermon has some bending "**their knees to God**" as they flee "**from the face of the serpent**" does not in any way prove, or even imply, that it was teaching that the church would still be in the world at that time.

So there is no reason to even question that the unknown writer of this sermon actually meant what he so plainly said, that "all the saints and elect of God are gathered, prior to the tribulation that is to come, and are taken to the Lord lest they see the confusion that is to overwhelm the world because of our sins."

Thus we see that the doctrine of a rapture before the great tribulation goes all the way back to the very oldest Christian commentary on Bible prophecy (of any significant length) which has survived to the present day, and that it continued to be taught at least until near the end of the fourth century.

APPENDIX

The source of J. N. Darby's
Dispensational Concepts

Anti-dispensationalists often claim that this doctrine cannot be truth because the origins of dispensationalism have a double taint. For they claim that J.N. Darby, who is well known to have popularized the doctrine and is widely (but incorrectly) thought to be its originator, actually got his ideas from a widely disparaged writer by the name of Edward Irving. And they claim that Irving in turn got these ideas from a Jesuit priest named Manuel Lacunza, who had written a book titled "The Coming of Messiah in Glory and Majesty." Lacunza had published this book under the pen name of Juan Josafat Ben-Ezra, claiming to be a converted Jew. Edward Irving had translated it into English and published it, adding a very long "preliminary discourse." And as Darby quoted from this "preliminary discourse," [80] and thus we know he read it, these people claim that this book is where Darby got the idea of dispensationalism.

But Darby himself clearly stated the source of his first understanding of dispensational concepts. Speaking of the prophecies of Isaiah, he said:

---

80 "Reflections upon the Prophetic Inquiry and the views advanced in it," by J.N. Darby, Dublin, 1829. From "The Collected Writings of J.N. Darby," vol. 2, {Prophetic vol. 1,} ed. By William Kelly, pg. 10, original ed. by Moorish, pg. 7, reprinted ed. by Stowe-Hill.

"But I must, though without comment, direct attention to chapter 32 of the same prophet; which I do the rather, because it was **in this the Lord was pleased, without man's teaching, first to open my eyes on this subject,** that I might learn His will concerning it throughout - not by the first blessed truths stated in it, but the latter part, when there shall be a complete change in the dispensation, the wilderness becoming the fruitful field of God's fruit and glory, and that which had been so being counted a forest, at a time when the Lord's judgments should come down, even great hail, upon this forest; and the city, even of pride, be utterly abased. That the Spirit's pouring out upon the Jews, and their substitution for the Gentile church, become a forest, is here adverted to, is evident from the connection of the previous verses." [81]

Further, in 1874, the famous church historian Andrew Miller, who is well know to have been a member of Darby's close-knit group, the Plymouth brethren, traced the beginnings of nineteenth century dispensational thinking in the following words:

"The study of prophetic truth was greatly revived in the early part of this century. In the year 1821 a short treatise, entitled 'The Latter Rain,' by the Rev. Lewis Way, made its appearance. The main object of the writer is to prove from scripture the restoration of Israel, and the consequent glory in the land. His poem entitled, 'Palingenesia,' or 'The World to Come,' appeared in 1824. Thoughts on the 'Scriptural Expectations of the Church,' by Basilicus, followed it in 1826. The author takes a wider range in this book than in the former, though the kingdom of Israel occupies a prominent place. In 1827 the Rev. Edward Irving endeavoured to arouse the professing church, but especially his brethren in the ministry, to a sense of their responsibility as to the truth of prophecy. He translated the

81   "Evidence from Scripture of the passing away of the present dispensation," by J.N. Darby, From "The Collected Writings of J.N. Darby," vol. 2, {Prophetic vol. 1,} ed. By William Kelly, pp. 165-166, original ed. by Moorish, pg. 108, reprinted ed. by Stowe-Hill.

work of Ben Ezra, a converted Jew, on 'The Coming of Messiah in Glory and Majesty,' with a long preliminary discourse. This book was originally written in Spanish, and first published in Spain in the year 1812." [82]

So Andrew Miller did not trace the origins of nineteenth century dispensational doctrine to either J.N. Darby or to Edward Irving, but to Lewis Way.

These anti-dispensationalists claim that J.N. Darby first became interested in prophecy through a series of conferences at Albury, which began in 1826. And as Edward Irving made presentations at those conferences, they take this as proof that Darby got his ideas from Irving. But in saying this, they ignore the fact that the conferences at Albury were not only also attended by, but in part organized by, Lewis Way, who also made presentations at these same conferences.

It is also critical, in tracing the origins of these concepts, to know that in his "Preliminary Discourse," Irving said concerning Lacunza that **"I do not find him so strong perhaps in the analogies of scripture and Providence, as the author of Basilicus and Palingenesia,..."** [83]

So we see that Edward Irving valued the works of Lewis Way. And earlier in this same work, he had said,

> "Now let this book be read as a voice from the Roman Catholic Church, and let the Palingenesia and Basilicus' letters of my friend be read as a voice from the Church of England, **and let the substance of my discourses for the last year, as given above, be read as a voice from the Kirk of Scotland;** and when the coincidence of sentiment and doctrine is perceived in the diversity of personal character and particular interpretations, let any one if he dare, reject the whole matter as the ravings and dreamings of fanciful men." [84]

---

82   "Short Papers on Church History," by Andrew Miller, London, G. Morrish, 1874, pg. 644.

83   "Preliminary Discourse," by Edward Irving, in "The Coming of Messiah in Glory and Majesty," vol. 1, by Manuel Lacunza, translated by Edward Irving, published by L. B. Steely and Son, London, 1827, pg. 19.

84   Ibid, pg. 15.

This statement is important as to dating the time when Edward Irving began to teach these things. For in this 1827 publication, he called his teaching on this subject **"my discourses for the last year."** This sets the beginning of Irving's teaching on this subject in the same year Lewis Way wrote the last of his three works on the subject. But it also shows that the year of the first Albury conference is when Irving first began to teach on this subject, while Lewis Way had already been writing about it for at least five years.

So, even assuming that Darby did indeed get his first dispensational ideas at the Albury conferences, which has been alleged but never proven, who is the more likely source of those ideas, the speaker who had been writing about them for the past five years, or a different speaker who first began to preach on this subject at about that time?

This is what makes a study of the dispensationalism taught by Lewis Way so important. Aside from this question, a study of Way's dispensationalism would only be an interesting historical detail. For Way's thoughts on this subject are not particularly elevated. And his writing style was awkward, to say the least. But he did indeed present a fully developed dispensationalism. And he presented it years before (or, in the case of his last book on dispensationalism, the same year as) the first Albury conference. And all of his works on dispensationalism were published well before either Darby or Irving had published anything on the subject.

As noted earlier in this book, the essence of dispensationalism is that, from time to time, God changes the way in which He deals with mankind. But that these changes have not been random, as it were trials, or attempts to find something that works. Instead, dispensationalism teaches that these changes have all been part of an overall program that God has had in place from the very beginning. So in view of this basic and essential definition of dispensationalism, we find that Lewis Way wrote:

> **"It will be readily admitted that a new aera commenced at the first appearance of Christ**, and the promulgation of the Gos-

pel, throughout the Roman Empire, the scriptural designation of which is 'the fulness of time.' This expression refers distinctly to the mission and personal office of our Lord himself: and the period which-thus commenced appears to be continued, without any marked interruption, to his second coming; **the whole aera being spoken of in this way by himself, and characterized by his Apostles under the general title of 'the last days,' in distinction from sundry other times, as the Paradisaical, Patriarchal, or Mosaic dispensation.** But **another aera seems to be expressly noticed, and it is specifically entitled 'The dispensation (or economy) of the fulness of times:'** under which, scattered parts will be gathered together; disjoined parts united in one great recapitulation of the whole mystery of God: when the detached and manifold gradations of the system hitherto in action will appear to have been working together towards one determinate issue, – the final scheme of man's redemption in body and soul, as originally conceived and planned in the eternal counsels of Jehovah: **when the whole creation, so long groaning and travailing in pain together under the corruption introduced by the Fall, shall be delivered by the power, and subjected to the dominion, of the Son of Man, the second Adam:** when the earth, once cursed for the sake of man, shall be blessed again, renewed, and fitter for the habitation of the righteous: **when the typical theocracy of the people shall be realized in the kingdom of Israel restored to the risen saints of the Most High:** when 'the Lord shall reign in Mount Zion, and before his ancients gloriously,' during the time appointed of the Father." [85]

This, without a doubt, is the very essence of dispensationalism. But many insist that a doctrine is not true dispensationalism unless it differentiates between Israel and the church. And some insist that it also requires a teaching that some will come to Christ after the end of the church period. So what did Lewis Way have to say about these things? First, as he tended

---

85 "Thoughts on the Scriptural Expectations of the Christian Church," by Lewis Way, London, 1826, pp. 30-31 in the 1828 ed.

to be rather wordy, it is necessary to make rather long quotations in order to actually show what he was saying.

Looking first at what Way said in 1824, that is, two years before the first Albury conference, he clearly taught that the dead in Christ would arise and **"the saints on earth"** would be **"caught up together with them in the clouds to meet their Lord in air"** when Christ would descend **"to judge the quick and dead."** He taught this as followed by a thousand year reign *on earth* by these saints, during which time the wicked would remain dead.

"The day of Christ's *appearance*, and his *reign*
When with archangel voice, and with the trump
Of God, he shall HIMSELF again descend
To judge the quick and dead. The dead in Christ,
Once quickened in their souls by faith in him,
Will then receive their bodies rais'd again,
And glorified, like that which he assum'd
When he appeared to Cleophas, made known
In breaking of the bread, and vanishing!
That white apparel, worn by those two men
Who spake of his return on Olivet,
Commission'd for the purpose; or the two
Transfigur'd with their Lord on tabor's mount,
Who then appear'd in glory; having on
Not this vile body, seat of sin and shame,
But garments like their Lord, of purest white,
Such as no Fuller on earth could make,
Transparent as the light, – **The saints on earth**
Rapt in a whirlwind, as Elijah was,
In pledge of their translation; will ascend
Caught up together with them in the clouds

To meet their Lord in air. – The dead in sin
Dead, shall not live; deceased, shall not rise,
Until the thousand years are finished.
Blessed and holy they that shall have part
In that Anastasis! The second death
Hath lost all power over those elect
Made like the angels who maintain'd
Their first estate, and shine as sone of God,
Then manifested heirs by sitting down
As Priests of God, with Christ, upon his throne,
According to his promise unto them
Who overcame by faith. **A thousand years,**
Thus shall they reign with him, and thus on earth,
For temporal reign in heaven there is none,
And this will have an end; for end will come
When even Christ himself shall render up
This kingdom to the Father, and become
Subject to Him, and God be ALL IN ALL." [86]

But concerning the restoration of Israel, in that same work he spoke of those who "confin'd salvation to their own exclusive pale! Exemplifying thus their ignorance of other unaccomplished mystery." He then went on to speak of the fact "That blindness, partial only, shall befall benighted Israel! – Till Gentile times draw to their end, and Gentile fullness come." And then he added, "Then out of Zion will come forth again the Great Deliverer, and will turn again ungodliness from Jacob – written thus and sure as everlasting covenant concerning them, and sealed with that blood which cleanseth from all sin!" Thus, he was clearly teaching that the time when "the Great deliverer" would "turn again ungodliness from Jacob," was after, not before, "out of Zion will

86 "Palingensia – the World to Come," by Lewis Way, London, 1824, pp. 91-93

come forth again the Great Deliverer." That is after, not before the Lord comes in power and glory to punish the wicked. This makes the eventual conversion of "Jacob," that is, Israel, after, not before, the time when the church will be gathered to Christ. For no interpretation of the timing of the rapture places it after the Lord has come in power and glory to punish the wicked.

"Great is that mystery, at sundry times
And divers manners manifest. The Word
Made flesh, and in the spirit justified,
Of angels seen, and unto Gentiles preach'd
And by the world believed on, receiv'd
Up into glory! Other part remains
Mysterious to the Gentile world at large
As once their first admission to the faith
And commonwealth of ancient Israel,
Was to the seed of Abrah'm; insomuch
That till the figurative sheet fell down
Full of all creatures – Peter scarce conceiv'd
A Gentile could receive the Holy Ghost!
How many that have stood in Peter's place
And sat as they presume in Peter's chair
Have held same partial doctrine! And confin'd
Salvation to their own exclusive pale!
Exemplifying thus their ignorance
Of other unaccomplished mystery
Which yet their true Apostle bids them know,
Lest self conceited wisdom puff them up,
That blindness, partial only, shall befall
Benighted Israel! – Till Gentile times
Draw to their end, and Gentile fullness come.

Then shall their fullness, as their fall before,

As their diminishing became, the riches

Of the Gentiles and the world.

Then out of Zion will come forth again

The Great Deliverer, and will turn again

Ungodliness from Jacob – written thus

And sure as everlasting covenant

Concerning them, and sealed with that blood

Which cleanseth from all sin! mysterious depth

Of wisdom! And of ways unsearchable

Past finding out! For who hath known the mind

Of God, or been his counsellor; save he,

The WONDERFUL, so call'd – the Prince of Peace?

Who saith 'I will return unro my place

Till they acknowledge their iniquity

And seek me in affliction!' They abide

As is written of them 'Many days

Without a king, a prince, a sacrifice,

Without an image, ephod, terraphim.'

Is it not written also 'Afterward

They shall return and seek the Lord their God

And their king David in their latter days?'" [87]

So, although he was rather wordy, in 1824, that is, two years before the first Albury conference, Way clearly taught that "**the saints on earth**" would be caught up and Israel "**shall return and seek the Lord their God**" at the time the Lord returned.

Turning now to his work of 1826, the same year as the first Albury conference, Way expanded and clarified these concepts. He said:

---

87   Ibid, pp. 106-108

"The first resurrection is thus immediately connected with the appearance, and kingdom, and coming of Christ 'with all his saints;' when 'he shall change their vile body (or the body of humiliation, σωμα της ταπεινωσως), that it may be fashioned like unto his glorious body' (Phil. iii. 21 —comp. ver. 10, 11): 'when he will present them faultless before his presence with exceeding joy' (Jude 24); 'holy, and unblameable, and unreproveable in his sight' (Col. I. 22): when they who are already risen in spirit with Christ, and are seeking those things that are above, shall also 'appear with him in glory:' 'when the *times of refreshing* shall come from the presence of the Lord.' (Acts iii. 19.) The expression in our translation of this passage falls far short of the original word, and seems only its secondary sense: if there be meaning in language, it signifies the times, or seasons, of RE-ANIMATION, restoration of the soul to the body; according to all analogy of diction." [88]

Here, Way could hardly have been more clear in stating that the resurrection of the saints would take place at the time when Christ appears.

Again, he also said:

"A review and comparison of the different passages of sacred Scripture which have a direct application to these subjects may suggest a somewhat different expectation; which is termed Scriptural, as being exclusively derived from the positive declarations of holy writ, taken from the original, in their most obvious and literal sense: the scope of which will be nearly as follows:—

That the present system, secular and ecclesiastical (as far, at least, as Christendom and the Roman and Mohammedan empires are concerned), will pass away at the close of a certain period or aera of the world, fixed in the determinate counsel of God, and so far revealed in his written word that its near approach may be anticipated, from specific and infallible tokens

88   "Thoughts on the Scriptural Expectations of the Christian Church," by Lewis Way, London, 1826, pp. 23-24 in the 1828 ed.

contained therein, whenever their real application shall be manifested by existing circumstances, and the palpable fulfilment
of the sure word of prophecy concerning the last times of the
Gospel;—**That a new order of things, and a distinct period or
aera of the world, will then commence, to which all preced-
ing times and dispensations have only been preparatory and
subordinate, and which is the perfection and consummation
of them all;—That the change thus effected in the physical
and moral, secular and spiritual state of the world, will be so
complete, so general, so extraordinary, as to correspond with
the nature and significancy of the expressions by which it is
exhibited in Scripture; such as, 'a new creation' 'a new earth,'
making 'all things new,' 'restoring all things,' &c."** [89]

Here, Way distinctly states "that the present system, secular and ecclesiastical... will pass away at the close of a certain period or aera of the world,
fixed in the determinate counsel of God," and refers to this end as "the last
times of the Gospel." And then he said "That a new order of things, and
a distinct period or aera of the world, will then commence." And in the
following passage he clearly taught that this would take place at "the coming
of the Lord."

"When Antichrist is destroyed, and Satan bound; when Babylon
falls, and the Beast and false Prophet are cast into the lake of
fire; **when the man of sin is destroyed, by the brightness of the
coming of the Lord; then, his enemies being made his footstool, all things will indeed be made subject: and then the new
earth and heaven, spoken of by Isaiah; then the new heaven
and earth, wherein righteousness shall dwell, expected by the
church, according to St. Peter; then the new earth, γη καινι, of
St. John, will appear: and this will not be εν τω νυν αιωνι, in
this age, but in that which is to Come, εν τω μελλοντι — εν τω
επερχομενω.** Into this οικουμενυ, God will bring his Son; **and
during this αιων, age, his saints will live again, and 'reign on**

89   Ibid, pp. 29-30

the earth:' and when this age of the world shall end, heaven and earth may pass away, but the word of God will not; for unto THE KING ETERNAL (of the ages) there remaineth 'honour and glory for ever and ever' (ages of ages), or throughout ETERNITY, properly so called. 1 Tim.i. 17." [90]

But then, Way went on to very clearly state that Christ's **"mission" "to the Jews"** would come at **"the second advent... of Christ."** This is therefore a very clear statement that the Jews would be converted after the church had already been gathered to Christ.

> **"The restitution of all things is connected with the second advent, or rather** *mission,* **of Christ to the Jews:** 'He shall *send* Jesus, which before was preached unto you (of the house of Israel); whom the heavens must receive until the times of restitution.' And thus saith the Saviour by Hosea (chap. v. 15), 'I will go and return to my place till they acknowledge their offence.'
>
> "'And so *all* Israel shall be saved; as it is written, There shall come out of Zion the Deliverer, and shall turn away ungodliness from Jacob.' (Rom. xi. 26.)
>
> "'The heavens and the earth were finished, and all the host of them: and on the seventh day God ended his work which he had made, and he RESTED on the seventh day' (Genesis ii. 2). And as in the third chapter of the Hebrews the Apostle is discoursing of the several rests of God and his people, he draws a due analogy between the rest of *creation* and that of *redemption,* and shews that they conterminate in the rest (Sabbatism) of the people of God: when they will not harden their hearts, as in the wilderness; and when they will enter into that rest which Joshua of old could not give them. The rejected state of Israel is spoken of in the language applied to the state of chaos, Jer. iv. 23: 'I beheld the earth, it was *without form and void;* and the heavens, and they had *no light.*' But when 'the captive exile hasteneth that

90   Ibid, pg. 37.

he may be loosed,' the Lord declares his purpose in the language of creation, saying, 'That I may plant the heavens, and lay the foundations of the earth, and say unto Zion, Thou art my people' (Isaiah li. 14—16). **And thus again the restoration of Israel is spoken of in connection with, or under the figure of, the new creation, Isaiah lxv. 17: 'Behold, I create new heavens and a new earth, and the former shall not be remembered nor come into mind: but be ye glad and rejoice in that which I create; for, behold, I create Jerusalem a rejoicing, and her people a. joy.'** It might appear by this passage, that the new heavens and earth are only a figurative expression for the restoration of Israel. **But the same expressions in St. Peter are clearly to be taken in a literal sense: he says, 'We look for new heavens and a new earth, according to his** *promise.'* **The promise referred to may be found in a corresponding passage, where the new heavens are spoken of in comparison with, and apparently distinguished from, the New-Jerusalem church:** 'As the new heavens and the new earth which *I will make* shall remain before me, *so* shall your seed and your name remain' (Isaiah lxvi. 22). **And this will be when 'the Lord will come with fire, and with his chariots, like a whirlwind' (Isaiah lxvi. 15); when 'he cometh out** *of his place* **to punish the inhabitants of the world for their iniquity.'** 'He hath promised, saying, Yet once more I shake, not the earth only, but also heaven: and this, Yet *once more*, signifieth the removing of those things that are made, that those things which cannot be shaken may remain.' (Heb. xii. 26; Haggai ii. 6, 7, 15; Isaiah xxvi. 21.)" [91]

Again, he said:

"The fact is, that by *opposing* passages of Scripture to one another, instead of *comparing* them, and thus observing their consistency and respective applications, we mutilate the character of both; cast them out of our hands, as it were, and break them to pieces, as Moses did the first tables of the Law: whereas, by

---

91   Ibid, pp. 43-44.

holding them up together, we may find them to be as consistent as the two parts of the Decalogue itself. For instance, compare Luke xvii. 20 — 30 with Luke xxi. 25 — 36, *oppose* or confound the kingdoms of God mentioned in each, and the whole is inconsistent: compare their relative application by the line of distinction between the two given in xvii. 25, and both are put in their places, and all difficulty removed." [92]

And:

"The kingdom of patience and the kingdom of power are here distinguished, as to the Messiah himself; and in chap. xxi. the distinction is extended to the disciples, and to the whole people of the Jews; 'They shall lay their hands on you, and persecute you;' 'Ye shall be hated of all;' 'In *patience* possess ye your souls ;' and, 'There shall be great distress in the land, *and wrath upon this people*, and they shall fall by the edge of the sword, and shall be led away captive into all nations; and Jerusalem shall be trodden down of the Gentiles, until the times of the Gentiles shall be fulfilled:' and 'then,' after certain prognostics of his approach, '*then shall* they see THE SON OF MAN coming in the clouds with power and great glory:' and after other indications, as clear as those of summer, which none can mistake, 'WHEN ye see these things come to pass, KNOW YE THAT THE KINGDOM OF GOD IS NIGH AT HAND.'

"Here, then, we find a kingdom of God which is not to commence, or to be nigh at hand, till the second coming of the Son of Man; and, therefore, as clearly to be distinguished from 'the kingdom of God within,' as a secret operation on the soul of an individual differs from an atmospheric phenomenon, co-extensive with the limits of the natural horizon, and discernible by every dweller on the earth. Consequently, these two kingdoms are not to be *confounded*, whatever may be their *connection;* and

92   Ibid, pg. 51.

that is truly very close and intimate, for none but the subjects of the one have any part or lot in the other." [93]

And:

"The kingdom in question is not to commence, as has been shewn, till the second advent, or mission, of Christ, at the restitution of all things (Acts iii. 18—26). Those things which God before had shewed by the mouth of all his prophets, that Christ should *suffer,* he hath so *fulfilled;* and of those times (when he shall come to reign) when he will restore all things, and, above all, the kingdom of Israel, "God hath spoken by the mouth of all his holy prophets." God promised to Abraham, that in his Seed 'which is Christ' (Gal. iii. 16), all the families of the earth should be blessed. He promised to David, 'I will set up *thy Seed* after thee, which shall be of thy sons; and I will establish his kingdom. He shall build me an house; and I will establish his throne for ever. I will be his Father, and he shall be my Son; and I will not take my mercy away from him, as I took it away from Saul,' — in whose person the Theocracy of Israel was first interrupted. (2 Sam. vii. 12, and 1 Chron. xvii.) These passages compared with Psalm lxxxix, Heb. I, Rom. I, and especially Acts ii. 30, shew that Christ and his kingdom, and not that of a literal David, was the great and ultimate scope of the promise.

"Accordingly Isaiah testifies the same in his most distinct prophecy of the Prince of Peace. 'Of the increase of *his government* there shall be no end, upon *the throne of David, and upon his kingdom,* to order and to establish it with judgment and with justice from henceforth even for ever: the zeal of the Lord of hosts *will perform this.*' (Isaiah ix. 7.) So chap. xxiv. 23; 'The Lord of hosts shall reign in Mount Zion, and Jerusalem, and before his ancients gloriously.' So chap, xxxii. 1; 'A King shall reign in righteousness, and princes shall rule in judgment:' and chap. I. 26; 'I will restore thy judges as at the first, and thy counsellors

---

93   Ibid, pp. 52-53.

as at the beginning: afterwards thou shalt be called, The city of righteousness.' So Jeremiah xxiii. 5, 6; 'I will raise unto David a righteous Branch; and a King shall reign and prosper, and execute judgment and justice *in the earth.*' **And this must needs be at the second coming of Christ, for it cannot apply to the first: 'In his days Judah shall be saved, and Israel shall dwell safely.' And the context proves, beyond dispute, that it is not on the return from Babylon, but on the last restoration of the Jews from 'all the countries' where they are scattered.** See also Jer. xxxiii. 14 — 16, proving the same position beyond all controversy.

"The xxxviith of Ezekiel, from verse 11, deserves the fullest consideration, as it contains the most comprehensive and conclusive arguments on the point. This having been already noticed, one more most remarkable passage shall be cited; namely, chap. xliii. 7: 'Son of Man, the place of my *throne, and the place of the soles of my feet,* where I will dwell in the midst of the children of Israel for ever; and my holy name shall the house of Israel *no more defile.*'

"So in Hosea (xiii. 9): 'O Israel, thou hast destroyed thyself, but in me is thy help: I will be THY KING.' So Micah (iv. 7,8): 'I will make her that halted a remnant, and her that was cast off A STRONG NATION; and the Lord shall reign over them in *Mount Zion,* from henceforth, even for ever. And thou, O tower of the flock, the strong hold of the daughter of Zion, unto thee shall it come, even the first dominion; THE KINGDOM SHALL COME TO THE DAUGHTER OF JERUSALEM;' and (v. 2), 'Thou, Bethlehem-Ephratah, though thou be little among the thousands of Judah, out of thee shall He come forth unto me who *is to be* RULER IN ISRAEL.' Thus in Zech. vi.12,13,of 'the Man whose name is THE BRANCH,' 'He shall sit and rule upon his throne, and he shall be A PRIEST UPON HIS THRONE.' And, finally, Zech. xiv, concerning the day of the Lord: Verse 4, 'His feet shall stand in that day upon the Mount of Olives, which is upon Jerusalem on the east.' Verse 5, 'The Lord my God shall come, and *all the saints* with thee.' Verse 9, 'AND THE LORD SHALL BE

KING OVER ALL THE EARTH.' Such is the testimony of Moses and the Prophets. That of the Psalms is general and clear, taking Psalm ii. as the key.

"Other passages might be adduced, but those have been selected which refer distinctly to *the regal dispensation of the Son of Man,* under circumstances not realized at his first advent —1st, The *salvation* of Judah and Israel. 2d, The *restoration* of the Ten Tribes. 3d, The gathering of the Jews out of *all countries.* 4th, The settlement of them in their *own country,* to be " pulled up no more." 5th, *The universal establishment* of Christianity. 6th, *The entire destruction* of the monarchies of the metal image, and the enemies of the church. 7th, *The unity* of doctrine and *uniformity* of Christian worship." [94]

And:

"This is a *terrestrial* state, for it is in 'a new earth;' and yet it is *heavenly,* for where God dwelleth there is heaven. It is a *temporal* state, for 'every one that is left of the nations shall go up from *year to year;*' and it is *spiritual,* because its object is 'to worship the KING, the Lord of hosts.' It is *legal,* because it is to keep the Feast of Tabernacles, which was a typical as well as commemorative institution of the *Law;* and it will be *evangelical,* because the Gospel, which now only commemorates the time when the Word was made flesh and dwelt in a tabernacle of clay (εσκηνωσεν), will then be perfected in the redemption of the body, the manifestation of the sons of God,—when the Saviour will no longer veil the majesty of his Divine Person, but be manifested in the glory of God his Father.

"The dispensation will be *local,* because 'in Jewry will God be known, and at Salem will be his tabernacle;' it will be *universal,* for 'all the ends of the earth shall remember and turn unto the Lord, and all the kindreds of the nations shall worship before

94 Ibid, pp. 56-59.

him.' (Psalm xxii. 27.) 'It shall be, that whoso will not come up, of *all the families* of the earth, unto *Jerusalem,* to worship the KING the Lord of hosts, even upon them shall be no rain' (Zech. xiv. 17); but 'the Lord will smite the HEATHEN that come not up to keep the feast of tabernacles; and '*all the nations* shall be *punished* that come not up to keep the feast of tabernacles.'

"To what period, it may be asked, of the legal economy, are we to look for the fulfilment of this remarkable prophecy? in what stage of the Christian dispensation have these circumstances been hitherto exemplified? Under the Law, no uncircumcised person had any lot in the commonwealth of Israel, nor communion with the ceremonial service of the temple at Jerusalem. The great object of those institutions was, to separate the descendants of Abraham from the heathen round about them, and from all the nations of the earth. Since the substitution of the Gentiles as the spiritual Israel and church of God, no pains have been spared by Christian interpreters to make out an almost exclusive claim to the blessings of prophecy yet unaccomplished; no dexterity has been wanting to shew, if it were possible, that the figures of the legal economy have already received their full and ultimate application in the spiritual ordinances and worship of the Christian church, as already established. Christ, it is true, is 'our Passover;' and the Feast of Weeks, is, or rather ought to be, spiritually transferred to the Christian Pentecost; but what authority is there for supposing that the festival in which we commemorate the first advent of the Messiah will correspond with the solemnities of the third great feast of the Jewish year, which, according to its final constitution in the word of prophecy, cannot be kept at all till the literal restoration of the Jews, and the local establishment of the kingdom of their Messiah?" [95]

And finally, as to our responsibility to evangelize, he said:

---

95 Ibid, pp. 70-72.

"There are two, and only two primary scriptural expectations prior to the great consummation. One is, the destruction of Babylon; and the other, the restoration of Israel. The *practical consideration* of these two would suffice, if duly enforced, to regulate not only the current of public opinion, but the course of Christian duty. It would give a specific and peculiar efficacy to those missionary labours, by which the remnant according to the election of grace is to be gathered in; it would accelerate the last universal publication of the Gospel, to be made, as 'A WITNESS,' to all nations. This, it appears, is intended rather for the *conviction* than the *conversion* of the world at large; for He who saith to his disciples, 'OCCUPY TILL I COME,' hath put also this practical question concerning mankind in general, 'When the Son of Man cometh, shall he find faith on the earth?'" [96]

This has been a rather long examination of a very wordy presentation. But it has been done to prove that Lewis Way taught, and clearly taught, although in a somewhat wordy fashion, not only the great outlines of dispensationalism, but that the end time expectations of the church and of Israel were entirely different, that the general conversion of Israel would take place after the end of "the Christian dispensation," and, in actual fact, after the Lord returns to this earth. Thus we see that Lewis Way was already teaching a fully developed dispensationalism before the first Albury conference, before Edward Irving began to teach on the subject, and before the writings of Manuel Lacuna were first published in English. And since Lewis Way was one of the organizers and speakers at that first Albury conference where Darby supposedly got the ideas of dispensationalism, the claim that Darby got his dispensational ideas from Edward Irving (whom he openly despised) is proven to have no merit whatsoever.

But what do Darby's own writings indicate as the source of his ideas? It was noted earlier that Darby quoted from Irving's "Preliminary Discourse."

96   Ibid, pg. 106.

But this quotation was part of a highly critical review of that document. [97] And later in the same article, Darby spoke very highly of a different earlier writer, saying, **"Another subject is the restoration of the Jews to their own land. The calm and judicious Lowth, in a day when nothing but the force of Scripture influenced him, could not withhold assent from the directness of the testimonies to this."**[98]

Here, J.N. Darby explicitly referred to the writings of the much renowned William Lowth, B.D., Prebendary of Winchester Cathedral. This man was born in 1661, just fifty years after the King James translation of the Bible was first published. He penned what became for many years England's most widely circulated series of commentaries on the Old Testament prophets. This included a commentary on Isaiah published in 1714, followed by one on Jeremiah and Lamentations in 1718, on Ezekiel in 1723, and finally on Daniel and the twelve minor prophets in 1726. These dates are important in comparison with the 1731 birth date of Manuel Lacunza, who, as we noticed earlier, is often claimed to be the original source of Darby's ideas. For this entire series was published before Lacunza had even been born. Yet Darby not only mentioned these works, but praised their author and commented that he had advanced the same ideas he himself was teaching.

So what, exactly, did William Lowth teach? Although his entire series of prophetic commentaries is easily available online, and in many large libraries, he said so much on this subject that we will limit our examination to the only one of them that can be downloaded free, so anyone can easily check the quotations given here, which come from Lowth's "Commentary Upon the Prophet Ezekiel," first published in 1723. [99]

---

97 "Reflections upon the Prophetic Inquiry and the views advanced in it," by J.N. Darby, Dublin, 1829. From "The Collected Writings of J.N. Darby," vol. 2, {Prophetic vol. 1,} ed. By William Kelly, pg. 10-15, original ed. by Moorish, pg. 7-9, reprinted ed. by Stowe-Hill.

98 Ibid, pg. 39, original ed. by Moorish, pg. 26, reprinted ed. by Stowe-Hill.

99 Available online at https://www.globalgreybooks.com/content/books/ebooks/commentary-upon-the-prophet-ezekiel.pdf

We will consider the different parts of Lowth's teachings, dividing them in the same way we did concerning ancient writers in the main part of this book.

So we will first notice that William Lowth clearly called various ages in which God related to mankind in different ways, "dispensations."

Concerning Ezekiel 20:11, he said:

> "... These Promises were made over to the Jews upon Condition of their punctual Obedience to the whole Law: *Levit.*xviiu 5. xxvi. 3, &c. *Deut.* xxvii.26. **And several Persons under that Dispensation are styled Blameless by reason of the Sincerity of their Obedience, tho' it was not Perfect or Unsinning :** See Luke i.6. *Philip.* iii. 6." (pg. 144)

And concerning Ezekiel 37:26, he said:

> "*Moreover I will make a Covenant of Peace with them,* &c.] See Chap, xxxiv. 25. The Words may likewise be understood in a spiritual Sense, **That God will be reconciled to them through Christ, and admit them into that Covenant of Peace, of which he is the Mediator, and therefore is called** *our Peace, Eph.* **ii. 14.** And then the following Words, *It shall be an everlasting Covenant with them,* may fitly be explained of the Gospel, being such a Covenant as shall never be abolished, **or give way to any new Dispensation.** Compare *Isa.* lv. 3. Jerem. xxxii. 40." (pp. 306-307)

We will now examine some of the places where Lowth spoke of literally interpreting prophetic statements of the Bible.

First, he said concerning Ezekiel 22:11:

> "*Which if a Man do, he shall even live in them.*] By Life is meant in the Old Testament all that Happiness which is contained in the Literal Sense of the Promises belonging to that Covenant: Comp. Ver. 25. and Deut. xxx. 15, &c. Psal. lxix. 32. Amos v. 4." (Pg. 143)

And he said concerning Ezekiel 22:21:

> "*I will gather you, and blow upon you in the Fire of my Wrath,*]
> God's Vengeance is often compared to Fire : See Chap. xx. 47.
> **But here it was so in a literal Sense, when both City and Tem-
> ple were consumed by Fire:** 2 Kings xxv. 9." (Pg. 170)

He further said concerning Ezekiel 28:25:

> "*When 1 shall have gathered the House of Israel from among the people
> among whom they were scattered,* &c.] **This, if we follow the literal
> Sense of the Words, is a plain Prophecy of the general Restora-
> tion of the Jews and their Return into their own Land,** as will
> appear, by comparing the Words with the Parallel Texts in this
> Prophet, via,. Chap. xi. 17. xx. 38, 41. xxxiv. 13. xxxvi. 24. xxxvii. 12,
> 14, 21, 25. xxxix. 27. and the Rules laid down concerning the Divi-
> sion of the Land among the Twelve Tribes, Chap, xlvii, and xlviii,
> do very much favour this Interpretation. Compare Isa. lxv. 9, 10.
> Jer. xxx. 18. xxxii. 41. in which Prediction most of the other Proph-
> ets agree with him: See the Note on Isa. xi. 11." (Pp. 232-233)

And finally, Lowth said concerning Ezekiel 34:25:

> "*And will cause the evil Beasts to cease out of the Land.*] This may
> be meant of Freedom from Persecution by Infidels and Strang-
> ers. Compare Ver. 28. Such a Security is elsewhere expressed by
> making a Covenant for them with the *Beasts of the Field*: See
> Hos. ii. 18. Job v. 23. Isa. xxxv. 9. Levit. xxvi. 6. **The Words are
> likewise capable of a Literal Interpretation, importing that as
> God had threatned that after the Desolation of the Land, wild
> Beasts should overrun it, and devour the few Inhabitants that
> were left, See Chap. v. 17. xxxiii. 27. So upon the repeopling of
> the Country, those Ravagers should forsake it.** (Pg. 284)

Again, William Lowth taught an end time return of the Jews to their
land. And he taught this so explicitly and repeatedly that it amounts to

insisting on that doctrine. Just tracing through the places he said it in this one volume will take many pages.

First, he said concerning Ezekiel 11:17:

> "*I will even gather them from the People.*] This may be in some degree fulfilled in those that returned from Captivity, **but the utmost Completion of this and the following Verses, must be expected at the general Restoration of the Jewish Nation.** See the following Notes, and Compare Chap. xx. 4. xxviii. 25. xxxiv. 13. xxxvi. 24. (Pg. 78)

Then he said concerning Ezekiel 16:55:

> "Ver. 55. When Samaria and her Daughters shall return to their former Estate, then thou and thy daughters shall return to your former Estate.] **When the Prophets foretel the General Conversion and Restoration of the Jewish Nation, they always join Judah and Israel together, as equal Sharers in that Blessing.** See Chap, xxxvii. 16—22. and the Notes there. (Pg. 118)

He also said concerning Ezekiel 20:38:

> "I will bring them forth out of the Country where they Sojourn, and they shall not enter into the Land of Israel.] See the Note on Ver. 35. The Word Country in the Singular Number may be equivalent to Countries in the Plural Ver. 41. The Sentence alludes as the former does, to the Judgment denounced upon the rebellious Israelites, that their Carcasses should fall in the Wilderness, and themselves never enter into the Land of Canaan: which shall be only a Portion for the Righteous among them. **This Text among many others favours the Opinion maintained by several Authors both Ancient and Modern, that the Jews upon their Conversion shall return into their own Land.** Comp. Chap. xi. 14. xxviii. 25. (See the Note there) xxxiv. 13. xxxvi. 24." (Pg. 153)

Here, Lowth referred to some of the authors presented in the main part of this book, as well as to some presented in the excellent book, "Dispensationalism Before Darby, by William Watson, which was referenced earlier in this book.

And he said concerning Ezekiel 28:24:

> *"And there shall be no more a pricking Briar unto the House of Israel,* &c.] My People shall dwell in their Land quietly and securely, when the rest of their ill Neighbours are destroyed: who were a continual Vexation to them, and as to many Thorns in their Sides. Compare *Numb.* xxxiii. 55. *Josh.* xxiii. 13. So a Thorn in the Flesh 2 *Cor.* xii. 7. Signifies a cruel Enemy or Persecutor, as appears by comparing that place with the Context, Ver. 9, 10. **The following Verse shews, that this Promise chiefly relates to the General Restauration of the Jews, when all the Enemies of God's Church and Truth are vanquished and subdued, often denoted in the Prophetical Writings, by the Names of Edom, Moab, and other Neighbouring Countries, who upon all Occasions shewed their Spite and ill Will against the Jews.** See the Note upon Chap, xxxviii. 17. and upon *Isa.* xi. 14. and compare *Jer.* xii. 14. with this place." (Pg. 233)

He further said concerning Ezekiel 34:12:

> *"So will seek out my Sheep, and deliver them out of all places, where they have been scattered in the cloudy and dark Day.*] I will bring them Home from their several Dispersions, whither they have been driven in the dark and dismal time of the destruction of their Country, and their own Captivity. Compare Chap. xxx. 3."(Pg. 281)

And he added concerning the next verse, Ezekiel 34:13:

> *"And I will bring them out from the People*, &c.] This Prophesie may in some degree have been fulfilled in the Return of the Jews from the *Babylonish* Captivity: **But seems still to look further,**

even to the General Restoration of the whole Nation; which most of the Prophets fortel shall come to pass in the latter Days: Compare Chap. xi. 17. xx. 41. xxviii. 25. xxxvi. 24. xxxvii. 21. xxxviii. 8. xxxix. 27." (Pg. 281)

He returned to this subject again and again, saying concerning Ezekiel 34:26:

"When I have broken the Bands of their Yoke.] The same Expression which is used concerning the Deliverance of *Israel* out of *Egypt*: *Levit.* xxvi. 13. *Jerem.* ii. 20. **Their Final Restoration being represented as the Greater Deliverance of the Two.** See *Jerem.* xxiii.7, 8. (Pg. 284)

And as an introduction to chapter 36:

"This and the following Chapter contain a Prediction of the general Restoration both of Israel and Juda, a Subjet often spoken of by this Prophet: of which the Return of the Two Tribes from Babylon may be thought an Earnest." (Pg. 290)

And concerning Ezekiel 36:8:

"Yield your fruit to my People of Israel, for they are at Hand to come.] This may have an immediate Aspect upon the *Jews* Return from *Babylon*, when they were restored to the Possession of their own Country. **If we suppose the Words to relate to the General Restoration of the Nation, the longest Distance of time that the Things of this World can extend to, is but as a Moment in respect of Eternity.** Compare *Heb.*x. 37. *Philip.* iv. 5. (Pg. 292)

And concerning Ezekiel 36:11:

"And I will multiply upon you Man and Beast.] As God in his Judgments threatens to cut off Man and Beast from a Land; See Chap. xiv. 17. So here he promises to replenish it with both. Compare *Jerem.* xxxi. 27. xxxiii. 12.

"Ibid. *And will do better unto you than at your Beginnings.*] In bestowing upon you the Blessings of the Gospel: the Promises of which were made first to the *Jews* and to their Children: *Act*.ii. 39. **The Words may likewise imply that God would give them a more lasting and secure Possession of their Land than ever they had before.** See the following Verses." (Pg. 292)

He said concerning Ezekiel 36:36:

"*The Heathen that are left round about you, shall know that I the Lord build the ruined Places,* &c.] The Heathen Nations that are near you, (See Ver. 4.) Shall be convinced that the restoring the *Jews* to their former State must be the immediate Hand of God, who will certainly in due time fulfil what is here foretold. See Chap, xxxvii. 14." (Pg. 298)

And as a general introduction to Ezekiel 37:

"**Under the Figure of a Resurrection of dry Bones is foretold the General Restoration of the Jews from their several Dispersions: and by the joining of two Sticks is represented the Uniting of Israel and Judah into One Kingdom.**" (Pg. 300)

And concerning Ezekiel 37:9:

"*Come from the Four Winds, O Breath.*] The Words figuratively represent the Restoration of the Jewish Nation from the several Countries whither they were dispersed over the World, expressed by their being scattered toward all Winds, Chap. v. 10. xii. 14. xvil 21." (Pp. 301-302)

And concerning Ezekiel 37:19:

"*They shall be one in my Hand.*] I will make them one Nation, and appoint one King to rule over them, the Messias. See Ver. 22. (Pg. 304)

And as a general introduction to Ezekiel 38:

"The Prophecy in this and the following Chapter concerning Israel's Victory over Gog and Magog without question relates to the latter Ages of the World when the whole House of Israel shall return unto their own land, Chap. xxxix. 25,26. And the Expressions we meet in this Chapter, Ver. 8 and 16. that this should come to pass in the latter Days, and after many Days, or a considerable number of Years, and that God had of old Prophesied concerning this transaction: These and other Circumstances of this Prophecy are a Proof that the Event was to happen a great while after the several Predictions of the Prophets concerning it. So that this must be lookt upon as one os those Obscure Prophecies of Scripture, the fulfilling whereof will best explain their meaning." (Pg. 308)

And concerning Ezekiel 38:8:

"*After many Days thou fhalt be visited,* &c.] This Judgment shall be inflicted by God upon thee, (Compare *Isa.* xxix. 6.) after a Succersion of many Generations: *in the latter Years,* or *Days,* as it follows here and Ver. 16. i. e. toward the end of the World, Compare *Dan.* viii. 26. Particularly the Expression of *Latter Days,* or Years is used to denote the Times of the General Restoration of the Jewish Nation. See *Deut.* iv. 30. Jerem. xxx. 24. *Hos.* iii. 5.

"Ibid. *Thou shalt come into the Land that is brought back from the Sword.*] The Land is put for the People of the Land, who are said to be brought back from the Sword, as they are elsewhere styled a Remnant, i. e. those that should survive after the Hardships they had suffered in their several Dispersions, and the Judgments that should fall upon the Disobedient in their Return Home: See the Notes upon Chap. xx. 54—38. and upon *Isa.* iv. 2. And perhaps those Words of *Jeremiah,* Chap. xxxi. 2. may be best explained to this Sense, *The People that were left of the Sword, found Grace in the Wilderness.* **The whole Chapter relates to the General Conversion and Restoration of the Jews, and** the Prophet speaks in that Verse of the Favours God would shew to those that should escape the severe Judgments that should destroy the Disobedient in their Passage home to their own Country, called the *Desert* or *Wilderness* by *Isaiah*, Chap. xl. J. and by *Ezekiel* the *Wilderness* of the People, or Nations, Chap. xx. 35. See the Notes upon that Place.

"Ibid. *And gathered out of many People.*] See the Note upon Chap, xxxiv. 15.

"Ibid. *Against the Mountains of Israel.*] See Chap, xxxvi. 1, 4.] *which have been always waste.*] Or rather, altogether waste, as the LXX rightly translate it.

"Ibid. But it is brought forth out of the Nations, and they shall dwell safely all of them.] Or, And they have dwelt safely all of them; the **future Tense** being often put for the Preter perfect. **The Sense is, that after the Return of the People of Israel into their own Country, and their having lived there for some time in Peace and Safety, this Enemy will think to take Advantage of their Security, and fall upon them unexpectedly.** Compare Ver. 11." (Pp. 312-313)

And concerning Ezekiel 38:11:

"*I will go to the Land of unwalled Villages,* &c.] . A Description of a People that live securely without any apprehension of Danger. Compare *Jerem.* xlix. 31.

"Ibid. *To them that are at rest and dwell safely.*] According to the Promise often repeated in the Prophets, that *In those Days Israel should dwell safely, and none should make them afraid.* See Chap, xxxiv. 28. Jerem. xxiii. 6. and the Note there." (Pp. 313-314)

And concerning Ezekiel 38:12:

"*To turn thine Hand upon the desolate Places that are now inhabited.*] Judea is described as a Country that lay desolate before the Jews return into it. See Chap, xxxvi. 34, 35. After it had been for some time reinhabited, Gog and his Associates designed to fall upon it with all their Forces; in that Sense *to turn the Hand,* is taken. *Isa.* i. 25. See the Note there. (Pg. 314)

And concerning Ezekiel 38:14:

> "*In that Day.*] **At that remarkable time, when God shall bring again the Captivity of Israel and Judah, so often spoken of by the Prophets.** See the Note upon *Isa.* iv. 2.

> "Ibid. *When my People Israel dwelleth safely, shalt not thou know it?* &c.] As soon as the News of their being settled in their own Country comes to thy Knowledge, thou wilt certainly make Prepartions to Invade them." (Pg. 315)

And concerning Ezekiel 39:9:

> "*And they that dwell in the Cities of Israel shall go forth, and shall set on Fire and burn the Weapons,* &c.] In token of an entire Conquest, and that such a lasting Peace should ensue, that there should be no more need of warlike Preparations. Compare Psal. xlvi. 9.

> "Ibid. *Seven Years.*] The burning the Weapons of War must be the Consequent of a complete Victory: So that the *Seven Years* here mentioned cannot be meant, as some would understand them, of those terrible Conflicts which the Jews had with *Antiochus Epiphanes,* from the 143d or 145th Year of the *Æra Seleucidarum,* (according to the different Computation of the Beginning of that Persecution. See 1 Maceab. i. 20, 29.) to the 151st Year of the fame *Æra,* when *Nicanor* was slain: ibid. c. vii. 1, 43. Nor is that true which this Opinion supposes, viz. that *Nicanor's* Death put an End to the Troubles of the Jews: for after that there was great Affliclion in Israel, the like whereof had not been since the time that a Prophet had not been seen among them, as the same Writer informs us, 1 *Maccab.* ix. 27. So that this Passage of *Ezekiel's* Prophecy must necessarily be expounded of some other Event." (Pp. 322-323)

But Lowth did not just teach that the Jews would be physically restored to their land, but that they would also be spiritually restored to their God. And again, he stressed this so often as to amount to insisting upon the point. So we see that he said concerning Ezekiel 11:19:

> "Ver. 19... *I will put a new Spirit within them.*] **These Promises chiefly relate to the general Conversion of the Jews: When God shall pour out upon them the Spirit of Grace, in order to their Conversion,** *Zech.* xii. 10. Compare Chap, xxxvi. 26, 27. and see the Notes upon *Jerem.* xxiv. 7. xxxi. 33, 34. xxxii. 39." (Pg. 78-79)

And concerning Ezekiel 16:61:

> "Ver. 61. *Then shalt thou remember thy Ways, and be ashamed.*] **The Jews shall be touched with a deep Sense and Remorse for their former Provocations, as necessary Preparation for their Conversion:** Compare Chap. xx. 43. xxxvi. 31. *Jerem.* xxxi. 9. 1. 5. and see the Notes upon those Places." (Pg. 120)

Again, concerning Ezekiel 20:40:

> "*For in my holy Mountain, in the Mountain of the height of Israel.*] In the Christian Church, called God's holy Mountain in allusion to the Temple at *Jerusalem,* built upon Mount *Moriah*: See the Notes upon Chap. xvii. 23. and *Isa.* ii. 2. The Prophet speaks here of the Jews as converted and united to the Christian Church: tho' **some Learned Men are willing to believe that upon their Conversion and Return to their own Countrey, certain Privileges shall belong to the Earthly** *Jerusalem,* **as the Metropolis of that Nation.** See *Isa.* lxv. 18, 19. lxvi. 20. *Jerem.* iii. 17. *Joel.* iii. 1 7, &c." (Pg. 154)

And concerning Ezekiel 20:43-44:

> "*And there shall ye remember your Ways and your Doings.*] The **Prophets suppose, that the Conversion and Restoration of the Jews shall be accompanied with a general Repentance, and a**

deep Remorse for their former Misdoings. See Chap. xvi. 6;. and the Note there...

"*When I have wrought with you for my Name's Sake*, &c.] When I have exerted my Power in your Deliverance, moved thereto not by any Deserts of yours, but purely out of regard to my own Honour, and the Promises made to your Fathers. See Chap, xxx-vi. 22." (Pg. 156)

And concerning Ezekiel 26:20:

"*When I shall set Glory in the Land of the Living.*] Compare this and the following Verse with Chap. xxxv. 14. When I shall restore other Cities conquered by the King of Babylon, to that flourishing Condition they formerly enjoyed among the Inhabitants of this World: to the Land of the Living signifies—Chap, xxxii 23, 26, 27, 32. The Word *Tsebi* is in many places appropriated to *Judea*, as being in several Respects the Glory of all Lands, Chap. xx. 6. but is sometimes applied to other Countries: See Chap. xxv. 9. **Some Expositors understand it here of** *Judea*, **to this Sense; that when God should return the Captivity of the Jews, and restore them to those Marks of his Grace and Favour, which distinguished them from all other Nations, and made them the nearest resemblance of Heaven that could be found upon Earth:**" (Pg. 208)

And concerning Ezekiel 34:23:

"*He shall feed them, and he shall be their Shepherd.]* This Prophesy was remarkably fulfilled, when Christ by the Preaching of the Gospel gathered in one the Children of God which were scattered abroad, *Joh.* xi. 52. *Eph.* i. 10. among whom were many *of the Loft sheep of the House of Israel, Matt.* x. 6. **But it will receive a farther Completion at the general Conversion of the** *Jews*, **when the** *Time* **will come that they shall say,** *Blessed is he that cometh inthe Name of the Lord, Matth.* **xxiii. 37. And this signal Event will usher in or complete the** *Fulness of the Gentiles*, See *Rom.* xi. 12, 15, 2 5 32." (Pg. 283)

And concerning Ezekiel 36:25:

> "Ver. 25..."Ibid. *From all your Filthiness, and from your Idols will I cleanse you.*] **When the Prophets foretel the General Conversion of the Jews, they usually mention their Detestation of their former Idolatries, as a necessary Preparation toward it.** See *Isa.* i. 29. xvii. 7, 8. *Jerem.* iii. 22, 23, &c. *Zech.* xiii. 1, 2. Some account of this Circumstance of their Conversion hath been given in the Note upon *Isa.* lxv. 7. and upon the Chapter forementioned Chapter of *Jeremiah.*" (Pp. 296-297)

And concerning Ezekiel 36:29:

> "*I will also save you from all your uncleannesses.*] I will take away the Guilt of them, and deliver you from the Punishments due to them. See *Matth.* i. 21." (Pg. 297)

And concerning Ezekiel 37:23:

> "Nor with any of their Transgressions.] **This Expression comprehends in it, their being touched with an hearty Compunction for their great Sin of rejecting and crucifying the Messias, their King and Saviour.** See *Zech.* xii. 10." (Pg. 306)

And concerning Ezekiel 37:28:

> "*And the Heathen shall know that I the Lord do sanctify Israel.*] **The Conversion of the Jewish Nation and their being restored to their former State of Favour and Acceptance with God, will be a Work of Providence taken Notice of by the Heathens themselves,** who shall join themselves to the Jews, as the Church of God and Temple of Truth. See Chap. xxxvi. 23." (Pp. 306-307)

And finally, we will notice one feature which William Lowth included in his writings, which was not included in any of the ancient documents we examined in the main part of this book. That feature is his repeated insistence that these doctrines are not just taught in the Old Testament, but also in the New.

So we find that he said concerning Ezekiel 36:26:

> *"A New Heart also will I give you,* &c.] See Chap. xi. 19. This Promise will be fulfilled, when the Heart of this People shall turn to the Lord, and the Veil shall be taken from it, **as St. Paul informs us**, 2, Cor. iii. 1 6. Compare *Jerem.* xxxi. 33, 34. (Pg. 297)

And concerning Ezekiel 37:12:

> *"I will open your Graves, and cause you to come out of your Graves.*] I will reunite you into one Body or Nation, who now lie scattered and dispersed as the Bones in a Charnel House. Compare Ver. 21. In their State of Dispersion and Captivity they are called the *Dead Israelites* in *Baruch*, Chap. iii. 4. and their Restoration is described as a Resurrection by *Isaiah*, Chap. xxvi. 19. at which time their *Bones* are said to *flourish*, or to be restored to their former Strength and Vigour, in the same Prophet, Chap. lxvi. 14. **In like manner St.** *Paul* **expresses their Conversion, and the General Restoration which shall accompany it, by Life from the Dead,** *Rom.* xi. 15. (Pg. 302)

And concerning Ezekiel 37:22:

> *"And one King shall be King to them all.*] The *Messias*, who is that one Shepherd and Prince that shall rule over them all, as one Nation: See Chapter xxxiv. 23,24. compared with *Luke* i. 32, 33. The *Messias* is described as King of the Jews in most of the Prophesies of the Old Testament, beginning with that of *Gen.* xlix. 10. concerning *Shiloh*. From *David's* time he is commonly spoken of as the Person in whom the promises relating to the Perpetuity of *David's* Kingdom were to be accomplished. **This was a Truth unanimously owned by the** *Jews*; **See Job. i. 49. to which our Saviour bore Testimony before** *Pontius Pilate*, **when the Question being put to him,** *Art thou a King?* **he made An-**

swer, *Thou sayest* [the Truth] *for I am a King:* **Thus those Words should be translated, for St.** *Paul* **alluding to them,** calls **them** *a good Confession,* **1** *Tim.* **vi 13. The same Truth** *Pontius Pilate* **himself asserted in that Inscription which he providentially ordered to be written upon the Cross: See** *Job.* **xix. 19-22. So that the chief Priests impiously renounced their own avowed Principles, when they told** *Pilate,* **That** *they had no King but Ceasar,* **Ibid. Ver. 15.** (Pg. 304-305)

And concerning Ezekiel 39:29:

> "*Neither will I hide my Face any more from them.*] I will never withdraw my Favour or Protection from them. See Isa. liv. 8.

> "Ibid. For *I have poured out my Spirit upon the House of Israel.*] There will be a new Effusion of God's Spirit upon the Jews in order to their Conversion: See *Isa.* lix. 20, 21. **a place applied by St.** *Paul* **to this very Purpose, Rom. xi. 26, 27.** Compare likewise *Zech.* xii. 10. and Chap. xi. 19. xxxvi. 27. of this Prophecy." (Pg. 326)

So we see that many of the essential concepts of dispensationalism were indeed taught, and very clearly and incessantly taught, by Wlliam Lowth, whom J.N. Darby praised by calling him **"the calm and judicious Lowth."**

In summary, what has been demonstrated in this book?

First, that all the following can be found in the very oldest surviving Christian writings concerning the subject at hand, and continue to be found in Christian writings from at least up to the fifth century, and are found again in Christian writings from the early 1700s and the very early 1800s, long before either Darby or Irving began to write:

- That the various ages in which God dealt with mankind in different ways were called "dispensations."

- That the explicit statements of Bible prophecy should be interpreted literally.

- That there is an unfulfilled prophetic program for the Jews.

- That the Jews will eventually be converted and restored to their God.

Second, both of the following are found in the very oldest Christian writings touching the subject at hand, and continued to be found in Christian writings at least up to the fourth century:

- That the seventieth week of Daniel's prophecy of the seventy weeks remains to be fulfilled in the future.

- That the church will be caught up to be with Christ before the great tribulation.

Therefore, the claim that dispensationalism was never taught before around 1830 has been thoroughly disproved. And the appendix has demonstrated that the claim that J.N. Darby got his dispensational ideas from Manuel Lacunza through Edward Irving is also unfounded.

DISPENSATIONAL
QUICKPRINT

Dispensational Publishing House is striving to become the go-to source for Bible-based materials from the dispensational perspective.

Our goal is to provide high-quality doctrinal and worldview resources that make dispensational theology accessible to people at all levels of understanding.

Visit our blog regularly to read informative articles from both known and new writers.

And please let us know how we can better serve you.

Dispensational Publishing House, Inc.
PO Box 3181
Taos, NM 87571

Call us toll free 844-321-4202

www.DispensationalPublishing.com